RENEGADE WOMEN *of* CANADA

The Wild, Outrageous, Daring and Bold

Marina Michaelides

© 2006 by Folklore Publishing
First printed in 2006 10 9 8 7 6 5 4 3 2 1
Printed in Canada

The Publisher: Folklore Publishing
Website: www.folklorepublishing.com

Library and Archives Canada Cataloguing in Publication

Michaelides, Marina, 1963–
    Renegade women of Canada : The wild, outrageous, daring and bold / Marina Michaelides.

Includes bibliographical references.

ISBN 13: 978-1-894864-49-7
ISBN 10: 1-894864-49-2

    1. Women—Canada—Biography. 2. Canada—Biography. I. Title.

FC26.W6M52 2006   920.72'0971   C2006-900368-8

Project Director: Faye Boer
Project Editor: Kathy van Denderen
Editorial Intern: Bridget Stirling
Cover Image: Kitty Rockwell, "Klondike Kate." Photo courtesy of Barrett Willoughby collection, 72-116-334, Archives, Alaska and Polar Regions Collections, Rasmuson Library, University of Alaska Fairbanks

We acknowledge the financial support of the Alberta Foundation for the Arts, the Canada Council for the Arts and the Government of Canada through the Book Publishing Industry Development Program for our publishing activities.

 Canada Council   Conseil des Arts
for the Arts   du Canada

 Canadian   Patrimoine
Heritage   canadien

Contents

Dedication

To my favourite mavericks, who know that
the greatest strength is in the tiniest little bit
and that peace and freedom are already within
and can never be fought for—
Ali, Ashoka, Benita, Bronach, Christopher, Cirra,
Diana, Dianne, Daisy, Ernst, Etienne, Eugene,
Gretchen, Jess, Jim, JdR, Kathy, Katrina, Karin,
Karla, Lois, Mariano, Mati, Padmaja,
Robert, Stan, Tessa and Zizi.
And Sam.

Introduction

YESTERDAY'S REVOLUTIONARIES BECOME TODAY'S TRADITION-alists and tomorrow's defenders of the status quo. Just ask a grandma who was once a teenager.

Rebellion is a necessary part of human evolution, and this book is the tale of many trails, blazed by women who braved the glare of public ridicule and private aggravation.

This is a collection of real-life sagas and dramas about women who didn't like things the way they were. So they changed them—sometimes intentionally in pursuit of their vision, other times by accident in pursuit of the truth and very often by design for the sake of equality. I have also included a few wayward women, just because, quite simply darling, they didn't give a hoot about what *anyone* thought of them and wouldn't have had a clue what to do with stigma even if it were served up on a plate for dinner.

You won't find in these pages women who have merely reached the superlatives of greatness, perfection, adventure or other stupendous heights of human endeavour. No. As wonderful as those women may be, these stories are about mavericks and rebels, shocking ladies and visionary women who have rocked the boat, pushed the boundaries and shaken up a cocktail of conventions that laid the status quo flat out on its self-important derrière.

Many of the women were wise and followed the integrity of their own hearts. Some were desperately wicked and followed the integrity of an empty stomach. Most of all, these chronicles are about women from all walks of life, from across Canada, from 1774 to the present day, who have lived by the saying, "Grant me the serenity to accept the things I cannot change, the courage to change those I can and the wisdom to know the difference."

Perhaps if we could take a little lesson from each and every one of them and mix them up together, we'd end up with the perfect woman. She'd be an all-singing, all-dancing, super-smart scientist-doctor, with an honesty no one could buy, who could fly a jet around the world, yet also survive in the remotest place on earth, where she'd have a game of pro-hockey just for fun and make an award-winning movie about it at the same time. She'd have the finances sorted out and would juggle these demands along with the kids and a hubbie at home. Without burning the dinner. And she'd still remember to feed the cat, water the plants and floss before bed.

They came, they saw, they conquered Canada and beyond. May the radicals amongst us follow in their pioneering footsteps.

k.d. lang
Ingénue Singer-Songwriter
(1961–)

I went in there understanding I was going in as kind of an oddball and that I was challenging the traditional expectations of a female singer at that time.

–k.d. lang

TRY SQUARING UP TO A COWBOY AND TELLING HIM YOU'VE got a really, really BIG beef against beef. Vegetarian k.d. lang did—and the cattle folk and country music fans came after her with their lariats let loose. Then she came out as a lesbian, and the conservative anti-gender-bending posse also took up arms against her.

Singer-songwriter k.d. lang actively courted controversy in a bid to remain true to herself and her artistic integrity. As a 22-year-old, just starting out on her career, lang declared, "I'm sure some people hate me, that's fine by me...until I sing their favourite song, then they love me."

k.d. lang's mouth has got her into as much trouble as out of it. For some, she has a national treasure of a voice and a rebellious, fiery heart. But to others, she's an outspoken, sexually politicized pain in the proverbial butt, with a pretentious way of spelling her name in lower-case letters that annoys the hell out of anyone with a spell checker.

❧◆❧

"k.d." stands for Kathryn Dawn. She was born in Edmonton, Alberta, on November 2, 1961, into a family of musically gifted children—two older sisters, Keltie and Jo-Ann, and an older brother, John. A year after Kathryn's birth, the clan moved to the tiny central Alberta town of Consort—population 650—where her father, Fred, bought a local pharmacy. Her mom, Audrey, was a schoolteacher.

At the tender age of five, Kathryn won a singing competition and knew this would be her life's work. Even though lang describes her childhood as secure and happy, it was obvious to everyone else that she was a rebel in the making. Her sister Keltie says, "From the beginning you never knew what Kathy was going to come up with next. She was full of the devil."

For lang, what others call devilish she just calls free spirited. Kathryn was a tomboy. By the time she was nine, she could fix trucks and take motor-bikes apart, and put them back together again. She'd always be climbing trees, and in quieter moments she'd dress up in outrageous costumes. She spent a lot of time with her dad, who taught her to shoot, and for a while the young Kathryn was Canada's second-best marksman. Or should that be marksperson?

Later in life, k.d. said her willingness to push boundaries came from the confidence she gained from growing up in a tiny community. "Fame is exactly the same as growing up in a small town— your life is an open book when you grow up in a small place. Eccentricities are normal. Everyone knows your business. It gave me a good training for being famous, for being so exposed."

But there was one bit of business that the whole town knew about while Kathryn's family remained oblivious: her dad was having an affair with the next-door neighbour. The Lang family found out the night Fred and his lover disappeared and never came back.

Kathryn was 12 and the only child still at home. She very quickly became the "man of the house," doing all the chores her father used to do, as well as trying to console her devastated mom. How her father's betrayal affected the young Kathryn and her future relationships with men isn't something the singer likes to talk about. She claims, now, to be at peace with her father, even though she has only seen him twice since, bumping into him once on the street when she was 20. He hardly recognized her and was with his new wife so made no attempt to rekindle the relationship.

Kathryn had her first sexual relationship when she was 13 years old, and it couldn't have been any riskier. Her first lover was the wife of a local schoolteacher.

"I knew it was wrong with someone who was married," says k.d., without any hint of regret. "I knew we had to keep it private. We had to sneak. Which is soooo sexy. I love sneaking. She [the schoolteacher's wife] was 23. I think she finally came out. Then I had a couple of lovers and then I had a high school sweetheart..."

Being gay seemed like the most natural thing in the world to lang. "I come from a family of four [kids], where three out of those four are gay, so it was extremely comfortable. I remember the moment my sister came out to me. We were dancing around the living room, she was on my shoulders, because she's very petite. She just said, 'I'm a lesbian...' and I said, 'Well, I'm bisexual!'"

Coming out to your siblings is one thing. The rest of the world was something else, and Kathryn soon realized the rest of the world wasn't ready for her news. At school she was cat-called mercilessly for openly mooning over her classroom sweetheart. Kathryn stayed in the closet publicly but plucked up enough courage to push the boundaries for her two gay siblings by admitting her own sexuality to their mother, who was horrified. "I'd rather be dead than have you tell me you're gay," she told her daughter. And later that year, Audrey heard the same tale from two of her other children.

"It was difficult for a couple of years," lang told *Chatelaine* magazine. "But she's [mom] really such an amazing woman. She's my mentor. She's 81,

but she never caps her knowledge." In the controversy that followed k.d.'s career later, she was
always torn between the pain her opinions might
cause her mother and her inability to compromise
her own truth.

After high school Kathryn enrolled at Red Deer
College and landed the lead role in a biographical
theatre production about the legendary country-
and-western-singer Patsy Cline. Kathryn was soon
head over heels in love again—with Cline. "She
was a very progressive woman who was trying to
make it in this [music] business. I guess I related
to her—the woman struggling against the odds."

What had everyone else struggling was
Kathryn's insistence that Cline had been reincar-
nated and was living inside her. Despite her
mother's warnings to the contrary, Kathryn
blurted out her Patsy fixation to anyone who
would listen, including the media who interviewed her early on in her career. Kathryn was
branded as a bit kooky.

Her rebelliousness was confirmed when she
dropped out of college without a degree. Even
though lang later acknowledged how useful two
years of voice training had been, she dumped the
rest of the course because she thought it was too
conventional and narrow.

Another thing Kathryn did was change the
spelling of her name to all lower case. She became
"k.d. lang." She justifies the name change by saying,

"I was influenced by the fact that my mother was a Grade 2 schoolteacher, and what I saw was usually in lower case, when kids are just learning how to write. And I remember seeing an e.e. cummings poster in high school. Plus it's a marketing gimmick."

As soon as she left college, k.d., as she was now called, named her first band The Reclines, in honour of her idol Patsy Cline. The band played gigs here and there, scraped by on meagre earnings and eventually managed to release a debut album, *Friday Dance Promenade* (1983).

But there was no love lost between the country music radio stations and The Reclines' new record. Many stations refused to play it on the grounds that the music was too avant-garde to fit into the traditional country music mould, and worse still, k.d. certainly didn't fit the mould of a country singer. Not only had she declared herself proudly vegetarian, but also her distinctly unfeminine attire of cowboy punk, big boots and cropped hair didn't sport a single rhinestone, and her sexuality became increasingly doubtful.

lang responded to the rejection by getting more eccentric on stage, using props, jumping around like a wild thing during performances and sometimes pretending to strangle herself with a microphone cord during a rendition of Cline's "Stop the World." But all this was getting her noticed, and it seemed nothing could stop her after The Reclines' second album, *Truly Western Experience*, won k.d. the Juno Award for Most Promising Female Vocalist of 1985.

lang accepted her Juno in a wedding dress and big black boots. One journalist commenting on the outfit said that k.d. looked more likely to stand on her man than to stand by him. It was great shock PR, and k.d. appeared in all the papers the next day.

lang's solo career, and her notoriety, really took off when she moved to Nashville and recorded three albums, *Angel with a Lariat* (1987), *Shadowland* (1988) and *Absolute Torch and Twang* (1989), the last of which earned lang the Grammy in 1992 for Best Country Vocal Performance, Female. For a while these albums turned lang into the hottest thing on the country music scene since hairspray. But although she won new fans with her loveable larynx, k.d. got stuck in the throat of all the traditional Nashville music fans. The Grammy was an insult to mainstream country aficionados, most of whom shook their heads at her overtly androgynous dress sense and the not-so-subtle meaning behind it.

Country music fans almost choked and eventually disowned lang completely when she appeared in an ad campaign for People for the Ethical Treatment of Animals (PETA) in which she declared, "If you knew how meat was made, you'd lose your lunch. I know—I'm from cattle country, and that's why I became a vegetarian."

The ad prompted such a negative backlash that
the Canadian Cattle Commission branded her as
a traitor. The reaction in conservative Canada was
so violent that someone sprayed over her hometown sign with "Eat Beef, Dyke." She got hate mail
and a flood of newspaper editorials. A boycott was
organized to ban lang's records from being played
on country music radio stations in Canada and the
United States.

It was lang's turn to be shocked. "The beef controversy hurt my mom quite a bit, I think. And it
freaked me out about controversy." On the plus
side, k.d.'s record sales went up from 250 a day to
1200 a day, and PETA received millions of dollars
of free publicity.

But by the end of this fiasco k.d. knew she and
the country music scene, where beef reigned
supreme, had to get a divorce. She took a sabbati-
cal from music to reinvent herself and starred in
her first movie, *Salmonberries*, in 1991. The movie
was packed with as many contentious social concerns as can be squeezed into a single full-length
feature. lang played an orphaned androgynous-
looking First Nations oil-rig worker who is trying
to find her inner self and her family as she simultaneously discovers she's a lesbian.

The critics who panned the movie said the only
good thing about it was the scenery—the stunning
Alaskan landscape—and k.d. in a naked full frontal
shot. What the rednecks back home in Alberta said

about the film is unprintable. What lesbians all
around the world began to say was, "let's watch
that movie again."

Next came round two of k.d.'s boxing match
with the establishment. In a 1992 interview with
Rolling Stone magazine, lang hinted at her "alter-
native lifestyle," and then finally, in an article for
The Advocate, she publicly declared herself a lesbian—one of the first major stars to do so.

Again, k.d. was torn. On the one hand she
describes the time as being "…a big moment in my
life and it was hopefully a very positive moment in
the evolution of gay rights." Yet on the other hand,
she knew her mother might suffer the consequences.

"…it's still something that people in that small
town where she lives are going to care about. And
that's gonna hurt our relationship. And that's why
I've always hesitated to be really, really out. It's
taken me a long time to say yes to *The Advocate*
because I know the repercussions are gonna be
there. It's like, I want to be out. I want to be out!
Man, if I didn't worry about my mother, I'd be the
biggest parader in the whole world."

Residents in k.d.'s hometown responded by taking down the town's sign that read, "Consort. The
home of k.d. lang." The sign had survived the beef
scandal, but not this.

Rejection bred creativity in k.d. Having been disowned by the country music scene, k.d.'s next
album, *Ingénue* (1992), was her first album of completely pop-oriented catchy tunes and dulcet bal-
lads. It was a hit worldwide and launched her as
a major international star and gay icon.

lang's status as the most-loved lesbian was confirmed when she made the headlines for her risqué
appearance on the August 1993 cover of *Vanity Fair*,
shot by famed photographer Herb Ritts. lang sits
in a barber's chair in male drag and is being shaved
by a swim-suited Cindy Crawford. Overnight, lesbian chic had become hip, and one journalist went
so far as to say of the picture, "It is arguable that
lang's image on *Vanity Fair* has never been rivalled
in terms of its gender-bending daring."

When asked about gender-bending, lang
declared, "That's my job! To transcend gender.
There have been many examples of performers
who do that—Elvis, Mick Jagger, Madonna. Art
transcends gender. As an artist, it's imperative that
you go right past the genitals and right into the
heart. That's my job, that's why I'm here, it's my
assignment."

lang's next album, *Drag* (1997), was a witty dou-
ble entendre of the title for the record where she
appears on the cover dressed like a very good-
looking guy in a three-piece suit. On the album
lang sings a collection of crooners about a subject

that got her into hot water with the ecology faction and the health conscious—smoking.

But, says lang, who doesn't smoke, "It's not really about smoking," she explains. "It is about addiction and need in all its different guises, whether that be love or tobacco...A cigarette is symbolic of life. It's very short-lived, like a love affair. You smoke it and it feels good temporarily, but it's killing you, or can kill you. Even though you know that, you go for it anyway."

By the end of 1997 lang became the most visible gay person in North America, and she moved to Los Angeles. She had trail-blazed acceptability of homosexuality at home and soon helped other big household names do the same. k.d. appeared as a coffeehouse singer in the groundbreaking 1997 episode of the ABC sitcom *Ellen*, starring Ellen DeGeneres, who came out as a lesbian on the show, and in public, in an art-imitates-life role. k.d.'s friend Melissa Etheridge came out soon after, and Roseanne Barr also declared herself a lesbian for a while, but then got married again for the third time a few months later.

By the time k.d. landed the role of a lesbian film director in the 2000 CBS miniseries "The Last Don," audiences didn't bat so much as an eyelid at her sexual orientation and made much less fuss about the positive portrayal of a gay character on prime time. k.d.'s hard work as a role model was paying off, and life finally seemed to calm down.

Even when k.d. had a much publicized five-year affair with singer Leisha Hailey, times had changed, and press comments about the couple were more curious than accusatory. lang describes the time as the best in her life. A new album blossomed from it, *Invincible Summer* (2000), which was as much a labour of love and tribute to it as her previous album *Ingénue* had been an ode to unrequited love.

Although k.d. and Leisha split six months after *Invincible Summer* was released, k.d. claimed that she was a different person. "In the past, I always chose to swim upstream. I'm kind of going with the flow right now, and it feels pretty good," she said. "I just feel a little less like I'm trying to prove myself, and a little more like I want to connect with people [the audience]."

And connect she did, and with a much older, pretty sedate crowd. The rebel who everyone's mom had loved to hate hooked up professionally with a singer everyone's mom loves to love—arch-crooner extraordinaire, Tony Bennett. Their collaborative Grammy-winning album of symphony-orchestrated duets, *A Wonderful World* (2002), was inspired by Louis Armstrong and was a far cry from cowboy punk.

k.d.'s latest offering isn't an album with attitude, but latitude. *Hymns of the 49th Parallel* (2004) is yet another musical departure for k.d. It's a return home that covers versions of some of Canada's most inspirational songwriters.

But while k.d.'s voice may have mellowed into one with a velvet vintage, her politics can still shock. She takes a radically different view on gay marriage than her traditional support base of liberals and lesbians. lang refuses to condone wholeheart-edly same-sex marriage on the grounds that mar-riage is a heterosexual notion that gays don't need to adopt. Traditional pro-family commentators didn't appreciate her opinions either.

These days, k.d.'s battles are more on the inside than the outside. She's become a Buddhist who is trying to fill a deeper existential void. lang summed up what she's coming to terms with in her life right now, "The problem is that people aren't representing themselves spiritually, so we keep digging for things materially to answer that, but it doesn't answer that need. It just perpetuates the cycle of suffering."

And looking back, k.d. has this to say on the question of whether she has suffered for her art, "The worst thing is that I used to be very social and very extroverted, and to preserve myself, I have become introverted and unsociable," she said in a recent interview. "I used to dress really funky and do crazy things in public, but now I don't. I try to stay as low-key as possible...[after touring and endless rounds of interviews] I don't want anyone to look at me and I don't want anybody to talk to me. I just want to be alone for a minute."

Going it alone, regardless of what anyone thinks, has been the guiding principle that k.d. claims has preserved her sanity in her 20-year career. She recognized early on that you'll kill yourself in the music business if you try to please all of the people all of the time. And some people will never be satisfied. At a concert recently, after she had hit a note of unmatched beauty, pitch, control and length, most of the audience swooned and some even cried out "I love you!" in stunned appreciation. One woman simply yelled, "Your hair's too short!"

CHAPTER TWO

Rose Fortune
Cop With Attitude
(1774–1864)

A CENTURY BEFORE THE LABEL "FEMINIST MOVEMENT" existed, Rose Fortune stood at the forefront of gender equality. Rose invaded the male world of policing and became the first-ever female police officer in Canada, patrolling the port of Annapolis Royal, Nova Scotia. Not only was she female, but she was also black.

Rose was born to slave parents in Virginia in 1774 and the family immigrated to Nova Scotia in 1783 along with other Loyalists, including 3000 blacks, after the American Revolution.

The blacks had been promised much in this new land. At least they were free in Canada, but discrimination persisted, and life was tough for everyone. Rose was a lass with strong arms and the initiative to match, and she soon carved a niche for herself working at the port as a "baggage smasher"—a baggage handler unloading heavy goods as well as transporting people from ships to their hotels in a wheelbarrow. As a sideline she started an early morning call service to wake up the persistently tardy in time to catch their next boat.

Rose was a colourful sight on the docks, wearing a man's hat, frock coat and boots, and a dress. She had a natural authority about her. At the time there weren't any police around, but there was constant trouble at the port. So Rose appointed herself to keep law and order. She imposed curfews and was even known to spank disobedient youngsters to keep them in check. Everyone listened to this tough, no-nonsense woman with arms and legs as strong as tree trunks. Under her jurisdiction, the docks were soon trouble free and running smoothly.

While Rose was prominent in keeping the law in Canada, she was also instrumental in breaking the laws of another country—the United States. Rose was an active member of the Underground Railroad, which transported escaped American slaves to safe havens in Canada and the "free" States in the United States.

Rose married John Francis of Digby, Nova Scotia, and they had two daughters, but the couple divorced soon afterwards. As a single mom she managed on the proceeds of her unusual career and her newly developed business acumen.

Rose started her own transport business, Lewis Transfer, in 1825, using horse-drawn wagons, instead of wheelbarrows, to move cargo and passengers. Owning and running a successful business was most unusual for a single black woman of her time. Her descendants took the business over after her death in 1864 at the age of 90, and they kept it going until 1965.

Rose's pioneering legacy lives on in her relatives. Her seventh generation descendent Daurene E. Lewis had originally considered becoming a doctor but ended up as a nurse because of the discrimination she faced. But Daurene, like Rose before her, eventually overcame society's prejudice against black women to command much respect from her community. In 1984 Daurene became the first female black mayor both in Annapolis Royal and in North America. She was made a Member of the Order of Canada in 2002 and was awarded an honorary degree from Halifax's Mount Saint Vincent University. Today, Daurene works actively on various company boards and is executive director of a number of charitable organizations.

CHAPTER THREE

Emily Stowe
Doctor Who Dared
(1831–1903)

*My career has been one of much struggle charac-
terized by the usual persecution which attends
everyone who pioneers a new movement or steps out
of line with established custom.*

–Emily Stowe, 1896

To EMILY STOWE, IT WAS A TRAVESTY OF DIVINE LAW.
Women were dying unnecessarily because modesty prevented them from being properly examined by male doctors. So Emily defied the law and
practised medicine without a licence. Having won
that fight, she went on to battle for political equality, setting the foundations for the suffrage movement in Canada that would ended in the "Famous
Five" from Alberta eventually winning the vote for
women and having the law changed so that
women could be "persons" under the law.

Emily, the eldest of six girls, was born in the pioneer village of Norwich, Ontario—into the sort of
life where a woman's work was hard and never

done. Her parents, who held strong Quaker beliefs, raised their six girls to believe in the principles of equality, education, integrity and independence.

Emily's mother home-schooled her daughters at a time when most girls had no education at all. By the age of 15, Emily was already unusual in that she started teaching at the local school and then decided to go to university. But the university turned her down because she was a woman—her first brush with institutionalized sexism.

Disappointed, Emily went to a teaching academy in Toronto, Ontario, instead, and earned a First Class Teacher's Certificate. She then accepted the offer of a principal's position at the local school in Brantford, Ontario, and became the first woman principal in Canada.

At 25, Emily gave up her career to marry, as was the tradition of the times. But when her carriage-maker husband John Stowe contracted tuberculosis and couldn't work, she went back to teaching to support their three children and pay the medical bills.

Teaching was the only professional job open to respectable women, but they were paid only half the salaries of men in equivalent positions. The justification was that men had to support families and women didn't—both unrealistic and ridiculous in Emily's case.

Although outraged by yet another example of blatant discrimination against women, Emily decided to choose her battles carefully because she saw that women faced much greater dangers than unequal pay in schools. She realized that the plight of women patients was a more important scandal.

In the Victorian era, it wasn't considered proper for women to discuss childbirth or even know about the human body. Decorum dictated that women had to be dressed when examined by a male doctor, which often led to misdiagnosis. And yet women weren't allowed to be doctors.

Emily was shocked at the consequent and needless suffering women had to endure. She had witnessed it first-hand during visits to her sick husband in hospital and vowed to do something about it—she would train to be a doctor.

She applied to the University of Toronto Medical School but was turned down because she was a woman. The men at the medical school argued that women were too delicate and lacked the physical strength to be doctors. They obviously had no idea how much strength was required to carry out the daily grind of washing clothes and hauling water, coal, groceries and children, along with all the other chores that women did.

Emily faced a gargantuan dilemma. The only place she could fulfill her dream was at the New York Medical College for Women. But it would mean leaving behind John and their children in the care of her sister so that she could be as equally "free to choose her vocation as her brother man, tethered by no conventionalities, enslaved by no chains either of her own or man's forging," she later wrote.

Emily forged on nevertheless. She went to the medical school in New York that did admit women. She learned homeopathic and allopathic techniques, and, after four years of study, graduated in 1867, the same year as Canadian Confederation. She returned home triumphant and set up her practice in Toronto at 39 Alma. It was soon so busy that an appointment to see her was hard to come by. But, suddenly, after all her hard work to get become qualified, a legal barrier came down on Emily that threatened to destroy her career.

An Act of Parliament was passed that made it mandatory for all doctors trained in the United States to take a matriculation examination at the Council of the College of Physicians and Surgeons of Ontario and to attend at least one session of lectures at an Ontario medical school. Without that, a doctor couldn't be licensed. And without a licence it was illegal to practise medicine. Practising without a licence was punishable with a huge fine of $100. Regardless, Canadian colleges still refused to admit women.

Emily wasn't about to stop practising medicine. The University of Toronto turned her down time after time, despite her letters to them predicting that "Your Senate may refuse to admit women now, but the day will come when these doors will swing wide open to every female who chooses to apply." The response she received was, "Never in my day, Madam."

This preposterous stalemate continued. "Dr." Stowe practised medicine unremittingly and was fined again and again for doing so without a licence.

But Emily's day did come. The University of Toronto Medical School finally relented in 1870. She and another aspiring female doctor, Jennie Trout, were admitted to attend lectures. The celebration was short-lived however. This period of study was the worst time in Emily's life. It became as much a study of chauvinism as it was of medicine. Every day became a barrage of sexist abuse— she and Jennie would arrive in the lecture hall to find rude drawings on the walls and severed, bloody limbs dumped on their seats. The two women stuck together and refused to be frightened into quitting. They decided to fight back in their own way.

It had become a popular pastime for the male students to compete with one another in recounting lusty and lascivious tales that had nothing to do with the day's lesson but everything to do with embarrassing Emily and Jennie into submission. Emily stood up to the lecturer and told him that if he didn't stop the students from telling these lurid stories she would tell his wife. The stories stopped immediately, and conditions in class improved.

With her studies complete, Emily had managed to jump her penultimate hurdle. But she still faced one more obstacle. Before she could finally practise medicine freely in Canada, she had to take her final exam before the Council of the College of Physicians and Surgeons—the one thing she needed to get her coveted licence to practise. Emily delayed taking the exam for a decade because she was convinced that however well she performed on it, the Council would be reluctant to pass her because of the trouble she'd caused. Her case had already attracted enormous amounts of publicity, and her practice was a roaring success—both factors that shook the medical establishment to its core.

While Emily procrastinated taking her exam, she continued to rock Victorian values a little bit further by supporting her husband in his training as a dentist after his recovery from tuberculosis. A woman? Paying her husband's way? Well, really! After John qualified, the couple set up a joint practice: she a doctor, he a dentist. They had a healthy flourishing surgery—despite Emily having to pay a few more fines.

In the end, Emily passed her medical exam and received her medical licence in 1880. She was 49. At last she could practise officially what she had already been doing unofficially for 13 years. Jennie Trout had received her licence a few years earlier, thus making her the first licensed female physician in Canada.

Dr. Emily Stowe had struggled for so long over education, medical training, licensing and professional respect—merely because she was a woman—that she had a stoic yet passionate yearning to obtain equal rights with men.

In November 1876, Emily founded the first women's suffrage organization in Canada. It was called the Toronto Women's Literary Club—an innocent enough sounding title that covered up the radical goals of an organization that aimed to overturn the legal and social status of women.

The women met weekly to discuss injustices and strategies to eradicate them. They effectively organized protests that led first to the statutory provision of separate washrooms for women in factories, and then later they persuaded store owners to provide chairs for female store clerks who would otherwise have to stand for more than 12 hours a day.

Next, they turned to politics. Emily was part of an 1881 deputation to the provincial government demanding the vote for women. In 1882 the women managed to achieve a small success when unmarried women in Ontario were granted voting rights on municipal bylaws, and then a year later unmarried women were also allowed to vote for representatives in municipal elections. But it wasn't much.

The Literary Club decided to come out of the closet in 1883 by renaming itself the Toronto Women's Suffrage Association. The label and the goal were loud and clear—equal suffrage for women. Within weeks, the women almost won that right. Prime Minister Sir John A. Macdonald was in favour and introduced a bill proposing equal voting rights for men and women across the country. The uproar was cacophonous. There were so many Members of Parliament (MPs) against the inclusion of women that the clause was dropped. Women had to wait years before becoming equal citizens.

Many of Emily's co-suffragists were becoming disillusioned with so much effort delivering so few results. Emily decided to reignite her sisters' rebellious zeal by inviting famous American suffragist Dr. Anna Shaw to Toronto. Dr. Shaw's speech was so rousing and persuasive that everyone was inspired to get back on board, with enough zest and vigour to create a new federal organization in 1889: the Dominion Women's Enfranchisement Association. Dr. Stowe became its president.

As the association's spokesperson, Emily had to reason against the arguments used to deny women's enfranchisement. Allegedly, females were neither intelligent enough to vote nor would they use their vote wisely even if they had it. Emily countered, "If the women of our country are not all prepared to use the newly imposed responsibility intelligently, neither are men prepared to use it intelligently. Of this I am certain, that the women of our country desire to use it only for their country's good."

Emily then organized a Dominion Conference in June 1890, which brought together women's groups from across Canada and the United States. The hall was festooned with banners declaring "Canada's Daughters Should Be Free" and "Women Are Half the People." The conference was a great networking success—a credit to Emily's perseverance for starting the federal movement in the first instance, and for keeping it going in the face of the opposition in Parliament.

The House of Commons was Emily's next target. It was her idea to stage a hilarious publicity stunt—a mock parliament in 1896 where the gender roles of real life were reversed. Women from the Dominion group played the role of members of the legislature, and it was up to the poor men of the country to beg humbly for the right to vote. The women threw back at the men all the silly and spurious arguments that men had previously used to deny women the vote: if men were given the vote they'd all want to wear women's clothes and do women's jobs, which would, no doubt, cause society to crumble. Men were designed for manual work and therefore should leave the evidently more capable females to run the country. And, of course, the Bible said men shouldn't vote either.

Every newspaper in the country featured Emily's PR prank.

In Ontario, the suffragettes had won a stalwart supporter in John Waters, a Liberal member of the legislature who put bill after bill before the House to give women the right to vote provincially. The male MPs derided him with contemptuous laughter, indignation and pomposity. But thanks to women like Emily and their tireless campaigning, the cause was very slowly taken more seriously and, at the very least, not dismissed outright as ridiculous.

As well as this mountain of political work, Emily simultaneously lectured, campaigned, persuaded and cajoled anyone who would listen to try to win the right of admission for women to the University of Toronto. She won her request in 1884, but it took until 1886 before the first female students were allowed to attend lectures.

Dr. Stowe also organized the backing of an influential group of citizens who got through reams of red tape in order to establish the Ontario Medical College for Women—the first medical school for women in Canada. The college was fully operational within a year, thanks to Emily's willpower, and it operated clinics where, at last, women could be treated by female physicians.

The college remained active until 1906 and was closed only because the University of Toronto, which had refused Emily so many times, finally opened its doors to women. Emily, however, did not live to see this momentous day.

Emily Stowe died in August 1903, one day short of her 72nd birthday, after a lifetime of breaking new ground for herself and all Canadian women.

This remarkable woman was a renegade, even in death. She wanted to be cremated because, as she told her eldest daughter, Augusta, "I have never done an act on earth to pollute it and I do not wish to do so in dissolution." But Canada's only crematorium at that time was in Montréal, and it wouldn't take the body, so eventually Emily's remains were sent to a crematorium in Buffalo, New York, and her ashes were then returned to Toronto.

Emily had become the first woman principal, the first woman to practise medicine in Canada and was the founder of Canada's first suffragette organization and the first medical school for women. The eminent "first" lady's legacy lived on in her children. Her daughter Augusta, who had seen her mother overcome frustration with deter-mination, felt that her mother's contribution to medicine was so important that she would follow in her footsteps. Augusta's path was easy in com-parison to her mother's. Augusta was accepted into the Victoria College Medical School in 1879, but this was more because the principal of the college was a close family friend, and had nothing to do with society's change in attitude. Augusta went on to graduate as the first woman with a medical degree from a Canadian institution in 1883.

Women were granted the vote in federal elections in 1918, 15 years after Emily's death, but without her, there is no doubt that it would have taken much, much longer.

CHAPTER FOUR

Penny Hoar
(Read the Poem and Guess
What This Woman Did for a Living)
(1952–1997)

I can't make a sound
remotely resembling a snicker
because I have to be quicker
with the flick of my whip
on the tip of their *****
their frenzy mounting
while I'm counting
the minutes and the dollars
they holler for mercy
no mercy

–*I'm a Damn Dom Now*, by Penny Hoar

NO, SHE WASN'T THE POET LAUREATE, SHE LIVED UP TO THE name that she was born with—a prostitute artiste, a woman with a thousand different occupations—but the one she did best was a cross-dressing dominatrix. Penny dressed as a man and thrashed lawyers, politicians, RCMP officers—any male in fact—who wanted to dress like a woman and get pounded. And they paid her a minimum of $100 an hour to do it. Often she got more than that.

"Lawyers always want to be abused, so I make them dress in a French maid's uniform and clean my house. Not bad, eh, getting $500 from a lawyer for the privilege of cleaning up my mess," she told *Toronto Life*.

Penny called this a "power inversion," a way to redress some serious imbalances in her clients' heads and nether regions. She liked to think of her erotic sessions as a therapeutic service. For example, one of her clients was a former white supremacist whose life changed overnight when he found out he was adopted as a child and was actually Jewish. His "therapy" was to doll up in frilly dresses, and it was Penny's pleasure to whack the living daylights out of him.

A typical guy-to-gal transformation from Penny started with a consultation on the look the client wanted—a secretary wannabe or a classic Holt Renfrew makeover. She had 200 outfits that Monsieur/Madame could choose from. Then she added an $800 set of false boobs, "a Victorian lace-up that brings them in four inches," false eyelashes, high heels and makeup to hide bristles—the works.

She filled her dishevelled house with full-length mirrors and claimed that "if there weren't full-length mirrors, there wouldn't be transvestites." As soon as she had dressed her clients to the nines, her men-that-look-like ladies would preen themselves in wonder at how good they looked with their new breasts and high heels.

Then it was time to play. Penny made mammoth paintings with feathers, an erotic tool that she and her clients rolled around on. She loved the way feathers glowed, and no doubt, after half an hour of that sort of romping, her clients glowed too.

This woman, who described herself as leading "A hyperactive life doing bizarre sh**," had a myriad of talents. She ran a restaurant called the Last Supper, which went bankrupt; worked as a costume designer for the nude theatre company l'Eskabel in Montréal; acted, modelled and danced her way around 18 countries; and set up a gigolo school in Acapulco. Some of her most notable performances included the unforgettable performance-art stripper characterizations of "Mountie Diddley Doright" and "Tammy the Tap-Dancing Tampax."

Not surprisingly, a lifestyle of this sort takes its toll, and Penny took a trip to the Parkside Clinic in Chicago to try to heal herself of bulimia, drugs and alcohol. She told *Toronto Life* that pop icon Elton John was also there at the time, and she found him "gentle and humble, stripped of grandiosity."

Penny loved the media attention she got for all her showbiz sex antics, so she upped the ante and became a media darling when she ran as a Rogue Rhino Party candidate in the 1993 federal election. The Rhino Party claimed to be the spiritual descendants of a Brazilian rhinoceros who was an elected member of São Paulo's city council in the 1950s.

However, the party's leader, Cornelius the First, was listed as a rhinoceros from the Granby Zoo east of Montréal. Why a rhino? Because, like politicians, rhinos are "thick-skinned, slow-moving, dim-witted, can move fast as hell when in danger, and have large, hairy horns growing out of the middle of their faces."

Penny campaigned for moving the Rocky Mountains one metre west as a "make-work" project, putting the national debt on Visa and adopting the British system of driving on the left—this last promise was to be gradually phased in over five years, first with large trucks, then buses and eventually small cars and bicycles.

But Penny's personal manifesto for the Rhino Party was a safe-sex platform. She promoted it in her campaign flyer: "I'm a condom activist; I want to equate safe sex with humour. Sure, it's life and death we're dealing with, but lighten up a little."

Safe sex and safety for sex workers seems to be the only thing Penny took seriously. She was aptly named "vice" chair of the Prostitutes' Safe Sex Project known as Maggie's, which she helped establish in 1986 to help streetwalkers become "loud, proud and empowered." Maggie's was the first sex worker–run education project in Canada, designed to educate women about health promotion, AIDS and sexually transmitted diseases.

One method to get healthy in Penny's mind was through "Sexercises," specially developed for "the female member," so she enrolled in a certified fitness instructor program later in life.

But Penny's exceedingly unhealthy lifestyle eventually caught up with her. She was found clinging to life with a needle still stuck in her arm after an overdose. Penny spent days in a coma, then, after years of abusing herself and others, died at the age of 45.

Her outrage at domestic violence and the pain of servicing her thousands of clients over the years is easily read between the lines of her poem.

> with the eons of oppression
> that has fuelled our depression
> of constantly being hit
> for being allegedly whores
> there are scores of righteous girls
> that hear that name
> before the fist comes screaming
> at their ears
> that's why I'm reaming
> to wipe away my tears
> at the years
> of being skewered
> by some dudes unconscious impotence
> ergo I go
> off to better things
> than bolstering their shrivelling thing

CHAPTER FIVE

Nell Shipman
Naked Starlet and Movie Mogul
(1892–1970)

Nature and her wild children would act for me…not as animated puppets but as living, breathing images of wilderness, purity at its divine source.

–Nell Shipman,
The Silent Screen & My Talking Heart

NELL SHIPMAN DID IT HER WAY. SHE SHOT TO STARDOM ON the silent silver screen, burned bright for a while but fizzled out of the limelight when her independent spirit was quashed by talking pictures and the Hollywood jet-set.

Canada's first female director was also an actor, writer, editor, independent film producer and animal rights activist. It was Nell who first used the expression "The Great White North"on one of the intertitles for a film, and the expression is still used today to describe the Canadian landscape.

Nell was a pioneer in pictures at the same time as the homesteaders were the pioneers of the prairies and before women could vote. Even though she spent only a few years in Canada, the feminist historians of the 1980s re-adopted Nell as the Canadian pin-up movie maverick of her era, the woman who forged the way for other women.

Along the way, Nell made a lot of really bad choices when it came to men. Her private life never lived up to her on-screen image of the feisty feminist heroine. She "married" four times, to guys who pulled her down rather than held her up, and she ended up dying alone and destitute.

"Nell" was the stage name taken by Helen Foster-Barham who was born in Victoria, BC, in 1892. Helen's British-born parents, Rose and Arnold, had settled in Canada a few years before Helen's birth with her older brother, Maurice. When Helen was 10, her family moved to Seattle, Washington.

On a visit to England when Helen was a child, she became stage-struck during a trip to the theatre in London. She set her heart on becoming an actress, and when a travelling theatre company came through Seattle a few years later, she convinced her parents to allow her to audition. She won the role of ingénue and, at just 13 years old, she set off in search of stardom.

Helen had to grow up fast. She changed her name to Nell and played vaudeville from Hollywood to Alaska and through to New York and Chicago. She was stranded more than once when a company went broke, and she had to hitch her own way home. Independence was a teenage necessity for Nell; her bravery, a blessing.

At 18, Nell was a leading lady on the stage and was snapped up by agent/impresario Ernest Shipman—"ten percent Ernie," as she was to call him later. If only she'd known then what she discovered about Ernest later. In her autobiography, *The Silent Screen & My Talking Heart*, written when Nell was 70, she described Ernie as "...one of the great cocksmen of his time, not immoral but amoral, not lascivious but lusty. If they named him dishonest, he was always within the law's fences contractually, and the ten percent he required of his minions' wages he considered a fair return for his efforts on their behalf."

Ernie was 21 years her senior and had already failed as a vaudeville promoter, but with Nell as his leading lady, some of his productions actually made a profit. He wooed and married her while they were on tour in 1910. Ernie lived off Nell's talents for years until she finally dumped him for another man.

Ernie was always on the lookout for the next big thing, the strike that would make him rich. He decided to make a break for the movies, and his ticket was Nell. The couple moved to Hollywood, where Nell landed bit parts in short films produced by Vitagraph, Selig and Universal. But at least she was learning all about the business. Then came the unexpected business of having a baby, which interrupted the couple's career trajectory.

In 1912 Nell took up writing magazine articles about the movies as a way to support them both while she was pregnant and couldn't continue acting. Writing screenplays seemed like a logical progression, but not a particularly lucrative one, because at that time screenwriters in Hollywood received scant recognition.

It was Ernest who "figured a day was coming when better-heeled motion picture makers would actually pay authors for the rights to their works," noted Nell in her autobiography. So she picked up the torch and, in various articles, including one for *West Coast Magazine* in 1912, criticized the studios for failing to include the scenario writer in a film's credits.

Just weeks after the birth of baby Barry, Nell "was thrown into the maelstrom of film writing," her articles putting food on the table until Ernie's next scheme got off the ground. Nell wrote screenplays for the next three years, as well as a novel, and then began to act again. *The Ball of Yarn* (1914) was Nell's first produced screenplay, in which she also acted. But it was so bad that even smooth-talking Ernie couldn't book it into theatres.

Nell's career really took off when she accepted an exclusive contract with James Oliver Curwood, a famous American writer of pulp fiction and stories about heroic animals set in the Canadian

North. He would give her exclusive rights to his stories if she would star in the films. The deal also gave Ernie the big break he craved—he would be the producer.

While Ernie thought about profits, Nell was the one who actually did the work. Not only did she write the films and act in them, but she also had a natural gift with animals. She tamed, trained and adored them, and she made them the stars of her films. Revisionist historians later claimed that Nell's affinity with these creatures, in real life and on celluloid, is symbolic of the heroine in action—one who tames the wild through nurture, not submission.

No other actor could do what Nell did with animals. In her autobiography, she describes a moment when, "I was acting with a free, large bear who might bite, hug or merely swat. She reared, put an arm about my waist, drew me close, gave me a tentative sniff, then licked my cheek, pushed me gently aside and dropped to the ground at my feet...All about us and within us was serene, untroubled, unquestioned. No personal bravery in this, just a fact of communication."

Nell's first movie with Curwood defined her early career. *God's Country and the Woman* (1916) created a passion in Nell for filming the wild outdoors, for real, at a time when location shooting was rare. Nell's remarkable outdoor photography became her trademark and contributed greatly to the popularity of her films.

But while big names such as Mary Pickford and Lillian Gish were becoming stars by playing wispy, victimized femme fatales, Nell was the opposite— her roles personified the strong, resourceful woman who comes through to save the day and, remarkably, usually ends up saving her man. Roles of this type became her trademark, and historians have praised them as the first images of the feisty female to hit our screens.

God's Country and the Woman made Nell a star overnight. She could have shot much higher, but she wouldn't compromise her choice of roles—or costumes. Samuel Goldwyn offered her a seven-year contract, but she had the nerve to turn it down because "I did not like the way they dressed their contract players," she said in her autobiography. Nell nearly gagged at the thought of being dressed as a curly blonde with a tiny lip-sticked mouth, covered from head to foot in yards of floating gauze material. She wouldn't be seen dead in anything other than a pair of mukluks and a parka. Or she would be seen with nothing on at all. Nell would bare all, only if she was going to profit from it.

In 1918 she set up an independent production company with Curwood to make *Back to God's Country*, a sequel to *God's Country and the Woman*. She wrote, co-produced and starred in the film, and she even did her own stunt work. Ernie raised the money from a Calgary businessman, and *Back to God's Country* was filmed in the frozen wilds of Lesser Slave Lake in northern Alberta in conditions so harsh that one actor died.

The film turned out to be the most successful silent picture ever made in Canada—all at a time when "nice girls" weren't expected to have careers. While the nice girls stayed home with the children, Nell's character Dolores was outdoors cavorting naked with a bear in a pond, with the nasty villain looking on from behind the bushes. This infamous scene from the film was Nell's idea. She originally filmed the scene in a flesh-coloured bathing suit, but she ripped it off when she saw how wrinkled it looked after the first take. The scene made Nell a superstar and goes down in cinema history as the first full frontal of a "star"— nearly 15 years before Hedy Lamarr's more famous nude swim in the 1933 film *Ecstasy*.

Sex sells. Just as effectively in 1919 as it does today. Posters for the movie featured a naked Dolores arching on tiptoes, and in the July 1920 edition of the trade paper *The Moving Picture World*, there was a warning to exhibitors: "Don't Book *Back to God's Country* unless 'You want to prove that the Nude is NOT Rude.'" The film cost $67,000 to produce and made profits of over $1.5 million. But Nell didn't see a cent because there was trouble brewing.

First, Curwood was furious that Nell had changed his story. In the original, it is the dog, Wapi, that saves the hero, but Nell edited the movie so that Dolores saves her wounded husband from the villain's clutches by rescuing him in a dog sled. Rather than compromise on the film or be forced to do so in the future, Nell declared her partnership with Curwood over. He warned Nell that it would be the biggest mistake of her life. She didn't care.

Ernie was livid, too, because his relationship with Curwood also died the instant Nell tore up her partnership agreement with Curwood. In the ensuing argument, it came out that Nell was having an affair with Bert Van Tuyle, the dashing production manager/actor, during the filming of *Back to God's Country*. The scandal made front-page news, which was fantastic publicity for the film, but too much for the marriage. Nell left Ernie, and Canada, to take up with Bert. She ended up without a single penny from the film, a divorce from Ernie in 1920 and the reputation of a woman as untameable as the settings for her films.

To say *Back to God's Country* was brilliant cinema is an overstatement. But Nell's film is the only notable silent movie attributable to Canada during this era, which is why many critics maintain that Shipman was a woman ahead of her time.

In 1920, riding on the wave of her success, Nell turned her back on Hollywood in an attempt to take control and set up her own production company, at a time when women had hardly any control over anything. She wasn't the only woman to set up alone, but the club was still tiny—Mary Pickford was the most successful woman to build a cinematic empire, and there were other notable women directors such as Alice Guy Blaché, Grace Cunard and Lois Weber.

Nell Shipman Productions was set up with "husband" number two, Bert Van Tuyle, as co-director. Although Nell styled herself as Mrs. Van Tuyle, no marriage certificate survives—the same goes for her two later relationships. Living with a man out of wedlock was scandalous if discovered, yet we'll never know whether she was naughty enough to take the risk, or whether it was just a case of once-bitten-twice-shy after her failed marriage to Ernie.

Nell and Bert made three short films in California, but they paid a heavy price for trying to make movies cottage-industry style. Independents were being drowned out by the fanfare and buying power of the newly emerging Hollywood blockbuster studios that produced, distributed and exhibited their own movies. The more Nell distanced herself from Hollywood, the more trouble she had financing her films. For the next few years money was so tight that when a film was finished, Nell put on a vaudeville-type show at the local hall to raise enough money to travel to New York where she'd try to sell the distribution rights.

None of Nell's films were profitable, but *Something New* (1920) was notable. Some critics called it a suffragette movie, because Nell's character is a champion driver who beats an embittered chauvinist male in a car race across the desert. The bigot lays down the challenge because a "crazy female" bashed in his fender the week before. But when Nell's character wins the race, he concedes that women should have "the right to vote and drive automobiles and do anything else they desire!" Yeah! First cars, next Parliament!

Nell did all her own stunts in the film and declared in her autobiography, "I have proven that woman is on a par with man in driving a motor car, as she is in every other walk of life. The ability is there. All she needs is the experience—the physical training—the freedom from restraint."

But as good as Nell was behind the wheel, she couldn't drive husband Bert to stop drinking any more than she could teach him how to manage money. Bert was the producer of *The Girl From God's Country* (1921), the couple's next joint venture, which went disastrously over budget. The film was also an unmitigated creative disaster. It was a convoluted epic in which Nell played two roles—twin sisters, one good, one evil. The film's backers made a desperate attempt to recoup their losses by editing the film from 12 reels to seven.

Nell was furious that her film had been tampered with. Fuming, she even urged exhibitors not to book it. The consequences of her self-sabotage were dire. "Was I blackballed from the business?" she later mused in her autobiography. "I really don't know for certain." What was certain was that the movie bombed, and she would never recover from it financially, or creatively.

Nell and Bert moved to Upper Priest Lake, Idaho, where Nell came up with the idea of building her own film studio, Lionhead Lodge, which housed her ever-growing menagerie of more than 100 animals. Nell may have loved the purity of the wilderness, but getting out in winter was a two-day dogsled and snowshoe trip across the frozen lake, often amid nightmarish blizzards. Bert suffered cabin fever and ran out into the snow, raving in delirium from frostbite, and Nell ran after him.

Nell was always hoping for a comeback, and she and Bert spent the next few years trying to recover from the massive losses incurred from *The Girl From God's Country*. But on her next film, *The Grub Stake* (1923), the distributor went bust, and she was penniless.

Life in Idaho had become a prison of "work and worry…debt and suffering," Nell cried in her autobiography, and the comeback never came. Creditors were suing, and a judge ordered her to sell her animals to pay her debts. Luckily, the San Diego Zoo stepped in and took all the animals.

Nell Shipman Productions folded in 1925, and so did her relationship with Bert. Nell devoted herself to writing for the rest of her life and had only one blip of success with a 1934 film called *Wings in the Dark*, starring Cary Grant. Her acting career was pretty much over, but Nell still had two more "marriages" to go.

She hooked up with artist Charles Ayers in 1925. The couple tried to make a go of it in Spain, where Nell had twins, Charles and Daphne, but Charles Sr. wasn't selling any canvasses, and the family went back to the United States where Nell found work as a writer. Charles Sr. couldn't cope with his failures, nor the humiliation of being supported by his wife, and their relationship of nearly 10 years ended in 1934.

But Nell wasn't alone for long, and she saved her worst man for the last. Amerigo Serrao had as many aliases as he had creditors. He was also a movie man, so the couple criss-crossed America together, trying to make their dreams of the next big blockbuster come true. By 1939 they were penniless and spending nights in the New York subway. Somehow they managed to pull through, though they were stuck in an endless round of picking themselves up after every failed venture.

The couple eventually made one movie in 1947—*The Clamdigger's Daughter*—but it was so bad it was never released. The cycle of near-comebacks continued until Amerigo's death in 1960. Forlorn, Nell spent four years of long, lonely bus rides visiting friends across the country until she went to live with her son Barry in California, who was doing very well as a screenwriter.

Nell's final project was *The Silent Screen & My Talking Heart*, her colourful and dramatic autobiography, which was finally completed when she was 78 years old. A few months later, in 1970, all alone in a tiny house in Cabazon, California, the woman who had been known as the "Queen of the Dog Sleds" died, ironically, in the desert.

Nell starred in 22 films, wrote 17 screenplays and two novels, and directed six films, produced five and edited two. Although she will never be remembered as a cinematic genius, Nell's colourful, rebellious life parallels the role of women in the first phase of film history—they did well in the free-for-all days of independent movies, and then got pushed out by big guys with big egos who did big business with big studios.

CHAPTER SIX

Rosella Bjornson
High Flyer
(1947–)

*If the fuel is low or the weather is down to mini-
mums, a woman is thinking about her baby, not
the safety of the passengers.*

–Off-the-record comment from a male airline pilot

WITHOUT WOMEN LIKE ROSELLA BJORNSON TO BREAK DOWN
the barriers, it's likely there would still be a massive no-entry sign plastered across the sky saying
"No place for a lady" underneath. When she
decided to become a pilot, Rosella knew it would
be a fight to take off, the turbulence would be
rough and there was no guarantee she'd land
safely. She had wanted four captain's stripes ever
since she could remember.

But Rosella navigated chauvinism, incredulity
and red tape with an understated manner that
kept her on course toward her indefatigable dream
to soar sky-high. She burned no bras or bridges.
She just got on with the job, juggled her career,
children and husband, and she never complained.
Rosella knew her every move was being watched,

and that all other women who came after her would be judged accordingly.

Rosella's dad had a private pilot's licence, and her flying career started while sitting on his knees playing with the controls as they flew around their farm near Lethbridge, Alberta. Rosella was born in 1947, the same year that Violet Milstead Warren became Canada's first female bush pilot. Rosella grew up flying, and her parents offered to pay for flying lessons for her 17th birthday.

When Rosella told her high school counselor that she wanted to be a pilot, "he just laughed and said that was impossible because I was a girl," she said years later in an interview. Rosella realized she had to be better than a man to get a job flying, so she went to the University of Calgary, knowing that airlines favoured candidates with degrees. While studying, she organized three flying groups, including the University of Calgary Flying Club. By the time she left university, she had officially clocked 500 hours in the air.

Rosella applied to every flying club in Canada for a job. Only one wrote back—the Winnipeg Flying Club. At least there was an offer of employment attached. As an instructor paid by the hour in the air, she virtually had to live at the club to make enough money to get by. By 1973 she had logged over 3000 flying hours and possessed all the commercial licences necessary for an airline pilot position.

She applied to all the major airlines, and every company said no—Pacific World Airlines (PWA) specifically wrote that they did not hire women. Rosella realized it would take a lot more than mere talent to get hired. She took a part-time job as a waitress at the Winnipeg Flying Club coffee shop where she befriended many of the pilots who hung out there. Through that grapevine she found out that Transair was hiring, so she walked right into the operations manager's office, without an appointment, and announced, "I want to fly for you." He looked at her aghast but told her to submit an application. An hour later the phone rang at Rosella's home, and she was offered the job of first officer on the Fokker-28, a 65-passenger jet.

With this job Rosella became the first female airline pilot and first officer in North America to fly a jet. Rosella admits she was, luckily, in the right place at the right time. Transair was just making the leap from a small bush airline to a passenger carrier; she had the backing of Transair's top pilots (who she had met in the coffee shop); no one could protest that she was too short at 6 feet; she had a degree; and the women's lib movement was beginning to shake up the patriarchy everywhere.

But getting the job was only the first hurdle. She then had to overcome constant ridicule and snide remarks as the only woman out of around

2800 Canadian airline pilots. An air traffic con-
troller once asked if Transair's first officer's jockey
shorts were too tight when he heard her high-
pitched voice over the radio. Some pilots at Transair
were disgusted with her appointment and jealous
of the publicity. The media hounded Rosella every
day. She had to take off to get away from them.

Rosella had planned to put her career before
romance, but she fell in love and married a pilot
in 1977. A year later, when their baby came, so did
trouble. The airline immediately grounded her on
medical grounds. There were no maternity leave
regulations for pilots, which meant she would
lose her benefits, job security and seniority. Then
the newspapers got wind of the story. Rosella
remembers the coverage: "My requests were made
to seem unreasonable and I was made to look like
a complaining bitch." She ended up taking a leave
of absence without pay in order to keep her benefits.

Eighteen months later, Rosella was back on the
job and thrown straight into a new course to fly
Boeing 737s. She hadn't flown for a while, the
course was tough, and her instructor made it clear
from the start that he didn't think she could make
it. And, as predicted by all those tough guys, she
missed her baby. But determination got her
through, and she passed the course. Now she had
to prove herself all over again to a whole new set
of pilots. One man in particular refused to fly with

her because he did not want to spoil his reputation as a male chauvinist pig.

He must have said a smug "told you so" when Rosella became pregnant again in 1983. Transair grounded her again, and the only saving grace this time was that there was no outcry from the press or other pilots.

Rosella got involved with Transport Canada to have the regulations changed so that a pregnant pilot could still fly "while under her doctor's supervision."

When she went back to work in 1987, it was for a new airline, Canadian Airlines International, which had taken over Transair. For the next few years she successfully juggled the various roles in her life with her steady diligence and soft-spoken matter-of-factness, until 1990, when she was finally rewarded with the four stripes she had dreamt of since she was a girl. She moved over into the left seat of the cockpit to become Canada's first woman airline captain.

◆

Rosella paved the way for Judy Evans Cameron, who became Air Canada's first woman pilot in 1978, and all the others after her. By 1995 Air Canada employed 20 women pilots. Today, the company employs approximately 80 female and 3200 male pilots.

Rosella still flies 737s for Air Canada out of Edmonton, Alberta, where she is the only female pilot. The plane she flies most frequently has a fluorescent pink livery.

Rosella was inducted, first in 1997 as a Member of Canada's Aviation Hall of Fame, and then in 2004 as a member of the Women in Aviation Pioneer Hall of Fame. A high flyer all round.

CHAPTER SEVEN

Ada "Cougar" Annie Rae-Arthur
Hunter and Homesteader
(1888–1985)

*She could be completely charming one moment
and totally hard the next—wily and conniving,
always scheming to make people help her. She was
incredibly selfish—I guess she had to be to survive.*

–One of Cougar Annie's visitors,
quoted in *Cougar Annie's Garden*

IF CANADA'S HISTORY IS ONE OF SURVIVAL AGAINST ALL ODDS
and a never-ending struggle to create civilization
from wilderness, then "Cougar" Annie's life is one
of the nation's most eccentric homesteading tales of
all, as well as one of the harshest.

Cougar Annie almost single-handedly eked out
a living for herself and her 11 children from a lus-
cious five-acre garden situated in the middle of
nowhere on the remote west coast of Vancouver
Island. Out of necessity rather than choice, Cougar
Annie survived by turning into a cantankerous,
fearless, "my-way-or-the-highway," stubborn
workhorse-of-a-woman.

For 70 years she held the reins, ruled the roost and laid down the law in her tiny far-flung domain, a kingdom she hardly ever left. Rumours spread quickly about her quirky lifestyle, bizarre business techniques and endless courage. The isolation of the homestead made it hard to separate fact from fiction, and Annie soon became a celebrated rogue, sometimes fierce, sometimes friendly, but always a force to be reckoned with.

Most of all, Annie became legendary as a hunter of beasts—and of husbands. She shot 72 cougars, 80 black bears, wild cattle galore and anything else that threatened her garden. She out-lived four husbands—and one of them, according to local legend, she actually shot.

Ada Annie was born in Sacramento, California, but she travelled more in her first few years than most people of that era travelled in a lifetime. She discovered her green thumb in Johannesburg, South Africa, then visited England, New Zealand and Australia before her family finally settled in Vancouver.

Her childhood was strange. Annie was brought up as a boy, and punished as one, by her strict, overbearing father, George Jordan, an émigré from Britain. He was often unkind and once taught Annie a lesson for a misdemeanour by tying her puppy to the back leg of a horse, which kicked the dog to death. He didn't want her to be sentimental, so he took away any animal she became attached to.

Annie's father kept her away from other children, never allowed her to wear girls' clothes until
she was nine and made her do all the hardest
chores to prove she was just as good as any boy.
George taught Annie to shoot when she was seven,
and she was a sure-shot by the time she was eight.
He also taught her to trap animals, totally unaware
that he was teaching her the skills she would need
later to survive.

Psychologically tough by the time she was a teenager, Annie was unemotional, self-contained and
wary of revealing any weakness, nor did she fear
any man—most unusual personality traits for
a woman of her time. But it would be a few years
yet before Annie could completely shake off her
father's controlling yoke.

When Annie was 20 she met William Francis
John Rae-Arthur, the black sheep of an aristocratic
British family. He was charming, intelligent and
a work-shy alcoholic. Annie's father considered
genealogy more important than bad habits so he
gave his blessing to the marriage, which took place
in 1900. She was 21; Willie was 36.

Willie's addictions soon spread to the fleshpots
and opium dens of Vancouver's seediest neigh-
bourhoods. His doctor warned him that it would
kill him. Annie had to get her husband away from
temptation. So, in 1915, the couple braved the
journey to Boat Basin, at the head of Hesquiat Har-
bour on Vancouver Island. The place was mostly

uninhabited and could only be reached by boat. It is notable for tempestuous seas, freezing mountainside mists and forests so strident that no other homesteaders to this day have succeeded in cultivating any land there.

The couple arrived with three children, a promise of a monthly income of 10 sovereigns from Willie's sister Isabella and Annie's heart and soul commitment to take care of her husband, her family and the land. The only reason they didn't perish the first year was because they already had a cabin constructed for them. If Annie had relied solely on Willie, they would surely have starved.

Willie was useless with his hands, but he could manage the arts. He liked to write, read stories to their children and play music, which was a fat lot of good when there was land to be cleared, water to be fetched, wood to be chopped, food to be planted, animals to be fed...the list is endless, but Willie's contribution was almost zero.

Whether Annie stayed with Willie because she had to or because she really loved this witty, well-educated layabout is uncertain. There is no record of her personal viewpoint, other than the fact that she stuck with him through thick and thin for the next three decades.

Annie worked for up to 16 hours a day, doing the work of two. But she was criticized up and down the coast for neglecting the children for the sake of the land she needed to conquer. She often left the children to fend for themselves, and even tied the baby into a highchair so that she could go out to work.

And the babies didn't stop coming. Annie gave birth to 10 more children in the 16 years between landing at Boat Basin and Willie's death in 1936. Eight lived. Added to the three she arrived with, her 11 surviving children were put to work as soon as they could walk—without shoes because there was no money to buy any.

The only useful thing Willie ever did was the paperwork that gained legal title to the land he and Annie had "pre-empted." Pre-emptions were free, large tracts of land that had the potential of being productive and arable. If settlers carried out the necessary improvements required by the regulations, the land was theirs.

The land was in Willie's name, but the sweat equity was Annie's—she spent her every waking moment toiling, and the homestead's success was because of her endurance and tenacity. During the 70 years that Annie spent at Boat Basin, other settlers came and went, and so did canneries, fisheries and logging outfits, but only her garden still thrives.

Once the back-breaking task of clearing a few acres of trees was accomplished, Annie planted her garden, which became her first love. She quickly developed a passion for flowers and turned it into a mail-order plant and bulb business that helped the family scrape by financially. Over the years Annie filled the garden with unusual specimens from all over the world, some of which reportedly shouldn't have grown under those conditions. Eventually, Annie presided over an orchard of fruit trees, a feast of flowers, vegetable gardens, chicken coops and goat sheds.

But as soon as her garden flourished, bears salivated for the fruits, and the cougars went into frenzy at the smell of Annie's goats. She dealt with the animals as mercilessly as she dealt with whimsical humans. She developed a complicated system of traps with a strategy to entice the beasts into them by tethering a lamb close by. Once the animal was caught in the trap, Annie blasted the creature to kingdom come. And made a profit of $45 a pelt.

Annie's reputation as a fearless trapper and cougar hunter became legendary. She claimed she never shot animals for profit, but rather, to keep them away from the family's only means of subsistence—the garden and the livestock.

Because Cougar Annie toiled dawn until dusk, it gave her licence, in her opinion, to take no nonsense from anyone. She was always on the lookout for the tiniest advantage in her favour, regardless of what anyone thought of her, and never gave an inch in business. Poverty made her tough and straightforward, though people thought she was just downright rude. She didn't think much of the area's Catholic church either, so she and the family never visited. For the locals, her wayward personality fed the idea of her rebel status.

The Rae-Arthurs barely made ends meet. Relatives sent care packages to help clothe the children. And Annie doggedly stuck to her promise to keep her husband away from vice. Visitors and neighbours were few and far between. The closest village, Hesquiat, was 10 kilometres away by boat. A ship, the *Maquinna*, regularly steamed up and down the coast, but there was no reason for it to stop at Boat Basin. And eventually, as the other homesteaders along the coast failed and left, the family became virtually isolated. But Annie was staying put.

After a rare visit to Boat Basin by government inspectors, the three eldest Rae-Arthur children were forcibly removed to a boarding school. Rumours had been circulating for years that the children were as wild as animals and were often uncontrolled, unwashed and unfed. To Annie, the children were just independent, and a little dirt never hurt anyone. Besides, she was far too busy to supervise their home-schooling correspondence courses.

It would be five years before the children could hug their parents again. Annie was adamant that she would not leave the garden. She was, however, much more vigilant with the younger children, who did do their homework and were therefore never sent away.

The paltry sums Annie made from the garden were subsidized by a series of wily deals and tricks. All schemes were Annie's in both idea and in execution—selling furs and eggs, raising guinea pigs, breeding rabbits and mink and running a grocery store. But then Annie wanted a post office, which she needed to ensure the survival of her flower bulb business.

She had to fight to get post office status, and "No amount of government red tape was going to stand in her way." She inflated the numbers of the local population so that their need justified having a post office. Years later, when hardly anyone came by anymore, Annie still bought stamps for the post office to keep up the illusion of demand, but then she'd convince other businesses to let her pay them in stamps for the goods she needed.

Annie's crafty ways were soon common knowledge. She disappeared when someone came to collect the cash she owed them; she bartered before handing over a single cent; she consistently sold people rotten eggs; and she charged different people different prices for the same goods, depending on whether or not she liked them.

For a woman whose life was turned upside down due to her husband's addiction, Annie idiosyncratically sold alcoholic vanilla extract because it attracted business. She was "fully prepared to take money from people desperate for a drink," says the chronicler of Annie's unusual life, Margaret Horsfield, and "fully prepared also to blame them for the problem."

Most people were happy to support the ramshackle store run by this lonely cougar killer, and unsuspecting visitors submitted to her insistence that they fix a fence, mend a wall or chop some wood before she would let them go. People could not say no to Cougar Annie—especially when she greeted them with a shotgun in her hand. Out in the wilderness she was never sure who was coming to visit.

In 1936, Willie, then 63, drowned in a dark storm off Boat Basin. Annie's monthly allowance from her sister-in-law perished along with him. Without the few customers from the post office and the store, she would have been destitute.

The one thing Cougar Annie never stopped shopping for was help, even if that meant having to marry it. Over the next few decades Annie snagged herself three mail-order husbands. Each time, matrimony started with an ad in the *Western Producer* that read, "BC widow with Nursery and orchard wishes partner. Widower preferred. Object, matrimony."

Husband number two, George Campbell, was a Scot of 60. Annie was 51. They married in 1940, but the couple shared precious little wedded bliss, or anything else in common. She just wanted a handyman; he just wanted the fortune he thought she possessed. George lasted a mere four years, until he allegedly shot himself while cleaning his gun. Most people believed that Annie pulled the trigger because she was no longer able to endure the beatings of a drunken Highlander who vowed to kill her unless she handed over her money. The police cleared her, but her fame spread.

Two months after George's death, Annie invited Esau Arnold to Boat Basin. Annie "auditioned" him for a year before they eventually got married in 1946. He was a simple farmer from Saskatchewan, not particularly bright, but a hard worker who was happy to serve. Because of him Annie could stay in her beloved garden—by this time all her children had left, leaving only the two eldest boys who came over intermittently to help with the chores. All went well at Boat Basin until Esau injured his leg felling a tree in 1954. The wound became gangrenous, and Esau was dead within a week.

With little time for grieving, Annie sent for Robert Culver, who was all set to become husband number four. Robert was a widower with two children of his own whom he adored and brought with him to Boat Basin for an "audition" in 1955. When Robert realized how isolated the place was, and that medical help was two day's away, he left, reluctantly, unwilling to jeopardize his children's health.

George Lawson answered Annie's last ad in the *Western Producer* and became husband/helper

number four in 1961. But just like the previous
George, this one also believed Annie had a fortune
but was too tight to give him a penny of it. However, unlike the previous George, this one got off
lightly. Annie drove him off the land at the end of
her shotgun in 1967. He never returned.

By now Annie was 79. She had no end of
willpower, still working more than 12 hours a day,
but her eyesight was fading.

She managed for a few years with help from
Robert Culver, who came back for frequent visits
until 1975, when his health could no longer toler-
ate the isolation of Boat Basin. He wrote to Annie
twice a week until her death; long whimsical love
letters, wishing he could be with her but regretting
the remoteness of the place.

Ironically, Boat Basin was finally blessed with
a road in 1974, a year before Robert made his final
trip to the garden. But it was a logging circuit road
that led nowhere, and the only journeys Annie
made on it were to the occasional parties at the
logging camp, where she was the guest of honour.
This stubborn old woman, untouched by the ways
of the world, entertained the men at the logging
camp with tales of hardship and courage, and they
in turn fell in love with the nearly blind, very batty
old woman. In her last years on the land, the log-
gers always looked in on Annie, fixed a fence here

and there and bought whatever they could from the store to help keep her going.

Cougar Annie hardly ever left her garden in 70 years. Even as a blind old woman of 80, her children all gone, she still had no intention of leaving the land. She schemed and plotted to be able to stay. She eventually took an offer from a friend, Peter Buckland, who bought the place from her on the condition that she could still live there. Peter also paid for two caregivers to look after her. "She was not an easy person to help," said one caregiver. Annie dictated all the rules and routines, made sure nothing went to waste, not even an onion skin, and point-blank wouldn't have things any other way than her own.

Annie spent her last few weeks on the land inside the house, unable to move, even though the garden still lived on in her head. She eventually had to be carried out at 93 years of age, tied to a stretcher so she couldn't stop them. She went to a hospice in 1983 and died two years later at the age of 95.

CHAPTER EIGHT

Frances Oldham Kelsey
Drug Enforcer
(1914–)

I think I always accepted the fact that one was going to get bullied and pressured by industry. It was understandable that the companies were very anxious to get their drugs approved.

–Frances Kelsey

SUDDENLY, IN THE EARLY '60S, BABIES WERE BEING BORN ALL over the world without limbs. Others had toes growing out of their hips. The list of deformities is as tragic as the number of "thalidomide" babies who have suffered—10,000 in total.

The numbers could have been even more horrific, but the drug thalidomide had not yet hit the U.S. market, due to the vigilance of Canadian-born Frances Kelsey. She was the new kid on the block at the U.S. Federal Drug Agency (FDA), just a month on the job. But she was smart enough and brave enough to stand her ground in the face of unrelenting commercial pressure, and she persistently refused to approve what has become known as one of the world's most dangerous drugs.

The case resulted in a revised code for the approval of new drugs and has forever changed the way medicines in America are tested, assessed and marketed.

⋘◆⋙

"I always knew I'd be some kind of scientist," said Frances, who was born in 1914 in Cobble Hill on Vancouver Island, BC. The girl had brains and graduated from high school at 15, going on to McGill University in Montréal where she was awarded a BSc in Science and, a year later, a Masters degree in pharmacology.

But jobs during the 1935 Depression were limited. "My choices were either to do graduate studies or to join the bread line. I decided graduate work would be more interesting," says Frances, with her characteristic good humour.

An employment offer finally came, but the letter, from a Professor Geiling in Illinois, was addressed "Dear Mr. Oldham," her birth name. Frances wondered if she should confess her gender, but she was advised to simply accept the post by letter and just write "Miss" in brackets after her signature.

"To this day, I do not know if my name had been Elizabeth or Mary Jane, whether I would have had that first big step up," says Frances. "And to his dying day, Professor Geiling would never admit one way or the other."

In 1937, Frances witnessed the horrors of putting drugs on the market before they were properly tested. She was part of the research team at
the University of Chicago that was investigating
why 107 people, mostly children, died after swal-
lowing "Elixir Sulfanilamide." Her tests showed
that it wasn't the drug that was killing the children
but the diethylene glycol in which the medicine
was dissolved—the chemical used in antifreeze.

Frances' work and the consequent public outcry resulted in massive changes to FDA drug
approval policy. For the first time, the Federal
Food, Drug and Cosmetic Act of 1938 put the onus
on companies to prove the safety of their products
and warn of any potential hazards before they
would be granted a licence to sell to the public.

Frances left the commercial labs for another
dose of academia. She obtained a PhD in pharmacology and then went to medical school, while also
bringing up two daughters from her 1943 marriage
to Dr. Fremont Kelsey. She became an MD in 1950.

In 1960 Frances took a step toward the history
books when she took a job as a drug reviewer at
the FDA in Washington, DC. Her first assignment
was supposed to be a straightforward rubber-
stamping of a sleeping pill called thalidomide. It
was also being widely prescribed to pregnant
mothers to alleviate morning sickness.

The drug had already been approved and distrib-uted extensively in Germany for three years, and in 46 other countries, including Canada, since the beginning of 1960.

The drug's manufacturer in the United States, Richardson-Merrell Company of Cincinnati, Ohio, claimed the drug was safe for pregnant women, was non-addictive, caused no hangover and wasn't toxic. After reviewing the file, Kelsey asked the company for more information—in her opinion their data was incomplete. She needed more statis-tics, a longer-term toxicity study and additional information on how quickly the drug was absorbed and excreted.

Kelsey was particularly worried about the absorption data, because 15 years earlier she had discovered that an ineffective dose for an adult could be lethally toxic for a fetus. She was also concerned that the company's tests revealed the drug sold as a sleeping pill didn't tranquilize animals, even though it did humans.

Every time Kelsey asked for more information and the company resubmitted its application, there would be a 60-day delay before the FDA was obliged to respond. The company was not happy. But they sent some of the additional information Kelsey asked for. It was not enough. "The clinical reports were more on the nature of testimonials," she said, "rather than the results of well-designed, well-executed studies."

The man in charge of getting the drug approved for Richardson-Merrell was Dr. Joseph Murray. He was not amused at yet another 60-day delay this upstart was causing, and he made endless phone calls to persuade her otherwise. Kelsey would not budge. She wanted proper trials. Murray didn't want to waste time or money.

Murray tried the personal approach, visiting her office, but when that didn't work, he complained to Frances' superiors, attempting to undermine her credibility. He claimed she was being irrational and unnecessarily hypercritical in a deliberate attempt to delay approval of the drug. Frances would not be bullied, even if it meant getting fired. She stood by her science. The company's proof was incomplete. And the FDA stood by her.

Over the next few days, Kelsey discovered the real reason for Richardson-Merrell's annoyance. "They were particularly disappointed because Christmas is apparently the season for sedatives and hypnotics (sleeping pills). They kept calling me, and then just came right out and said, 'We want to get this drug on the market before Christmas, because that is when our best sales are.'"

Then came a bombshell from London. *The British Medical Journal*, one of the most prestigious medical publications in the world, published a letter from a doctor who described serious side effects in patients who took thalidomide over a long period;

in particular, symptoms that included a painful tin-
gling in the arms and feet.

Having read the letter, Kelsey knew her previous hunch was a nightmare come true—she was
now seriously worried about thalidomide's effect
on the unborn babies of pregnant mothers for whom
the drug had been specifically targeted for morning
sickness.

She wrote to Murray asking for proof that the
drug would not affect the nerves of a developing
fetus. Kelsey's timing was grim. Before Murray
replied, reports flooded in from European doctors of
a wave of babies born with flipper-like arms or no
limbs at all. Toes appeared where knees should be,
internal organs were malformed, and worst of all,
there was a massive 30% increase in miscarriages,
stillborns or babies who died soon after birth.

In November 1961, 16 months after Richardson-
Merrell had originally applied for approval of
thalidomide in the United States, and Kelsey had
consistently refused to give it, a German doctor
conclusively linked the wave of birth defects to
pregnant mothers who took thalidomide in their
first three months of pregnancy.

Ten days later, health authorities took the drug
off the market in Germany, against the wishes of
the manufacturer, Chemie Grunenthal. It took
three more months for the drug to be withdrawn
in Canada.

Despite the growing evidence, Richardson-Merrell kept up its application to the FDA for another four months, until March 1962. Kelsey kept turning it down.

Kelsey's stubborn skepticism meant that only 17 children in the United States suffered the same fate as the 10,000 not-so-lucky children worldwide. Numbers in Canada were estimated to be around 150.

When the American public woke up to the fact that it was only Kelsey's professionalism that had averted a catastrophe, the resulting furor was the impetus for an amendment to the drug-testing law of 1938, a change which Kelsey was instrumental in creating. In the Kefauver-Harris Amendment dated October 19, 1962, companies had to prove that drugs were not only safe, but actually effective, and informed consent was required of any humans involved in experiments.

Frances Kelsey was not a visionary but a committed perfectionist whose concern for public health was responsible for the two most important pieces of U.S. legislation regarding the testing of drugs. She was appointed the head of the newly created investigational drug branch at the FDA, and in 1962 President Kennedy awarded her the Distinguished Federal Civilian Service Medal, the highest honour that can be bestowed on a civilian in the United States.

At the age of 86 Frances was still working as deputy of scientific and medical affairs at the Center for Drug Evaluation and Research in the U.S. She plays a major role in the ongoing debate about whether or not to fast-track drugs through the FDA protocols for "last-resort" patients, such as those with HIV, who are likely to die before potentially life-saving drugs are tested and approved.

The Canadians affected by thalidomide were each granted out-of-court settlements of about $200,000 when the case was first settled against Richardson-Merrell. But a federal task force also found the government partly responsible for licensing the drug without adequate evidence and awarded them a further $8.5 million in 1991.

Thalidomide was approved in 1998 for the treatment of leprosy, some HIV-related diseases and cancers, but only under the strictest of conditions. To date, it is the most heavily regulated drug in U.S. history.

CHAPTER NINE

Pearl Hart
Outlaw
(1871–??)

The sun was shining brightly
On a pleasant afternoon.
My partner speaking lightly,
said the stage would be here soon.
We saw it coming around the bend
and called to them to halt.
Then to their pockets we did attend.
If they got hurt, 'twas their own fault.

–Extract of a poem by Pearl Hart

IN THE LAST DAYS OF THE WILD, WILD WEST, THE LAST-EVER stagecoach robbery in history was not the brain-child of some Clint Eastwood look-alike on his last legs. Although it is true that the felon who committed the world's last holdup was a foul-mouthed, cigar-smoking desperado who had fallen on hard times, any other similarities with Clint end there. The outlaw was a rather young, quite chubby and very female Canadian.

Pearl Hart became notorious as a bandit queen and jail-breaker. She didn't steal much cash, yet she stole the public's imagination with romantic tales of woe, the lawmaker's patience with the ineptitude of her crimes and the publicity that followed her wherever she went.

Pearl didn't start out as a rotten apple, nor was she ever considered a juicy-looking peach. But she certainly lived a fruity, out of the ordinary kind of life. Bitter, sweet and ultimately ripe for a big fall.

Very little is known about Pearl's early life other than she was born into a well-to-do middle-class Ontario family. She was described as a friendly and outgoing teenager who rarely turned down a date. But any hopes of marrying respectably were dashed when, while at boarding school, she met a dastardly yet dashing braggart named Frederick Hart. They eloped.

Fred turned out to be a work-shy, wife-beating, gambling alcoholic. Pearl put up with it for a while, but on a trip to a fair in Chicago, while Fred was lost in the gambling dens, she fell in love anew. She was smitten by a Wild West show. She went back to watch it day after day, besotted by the image of such a romantic lifestyle and obsessed with the cowboys' masculinity—everything her useless husband wasn't.

So Pearl dumped Fred and headed out west— a brave move for a Victorian girl of her class who was also six months pregnant. In Colorado, she shocked the locals by giving birth to a son but then escaped the stigma of single motherhood by taking him back to Canada to live with her mother.

Pearl was free to roam once more and tried to make it in Arizona, but the drudgery of menial low-paying cooking and cleaning jobs meant her romantic dreams of the West were fading fast. When Fred caught up with her again and convinced her he'd get a job and support them both, Pearl jumped at it. The couple played happy family for a while, and a daughter was born in 1895.

But Fred simply couldn't stick sedate family life, and when his daughter was three years old, he left to join the army. As a parting gift, he beat poor Pearl unconscious.

Pearl picked up another boyfriend, Joe Boot, in 1899 when she worked as a cook in a mining camp. He wanted to marry her, but she wasn't about to repeat the horrors of matrimony. Pearl's next nightmare arrived in the form of a letter—her mother was desperately ill and needed money for medical care. Pearl and Joe sent her whatever minimal savings they had and then tried a couple of business ventures, but both failed miserably.

Pearl's increasing desperation and her mother's deteriorating condition got Joe to thinking about how to make a lot of money, quick—legal or not. He came up with the idea of robbing America's last remaining stagecoach, which covered the 97 kilometre journey from Globe to Florence, two towns near Phoenix, Arizona.

Joe thought the stickup would be easy. It had been so long since anyone had actually robbed a stagecoach that it no longer had anyone riding shotgun to protect the passengers. Pearl eventually agreed to the plan, cut her hair short, dressed like a cowboy and rode out with her accomplice to lie in wait at a bend in the road, where they knew the coach had to slow down and they could jump it.

On May 30, 1899, the two bandits leapt on board the coach and brought it to a screeching halt. While Joe covered her back, Pearl grabbed the driver's gun and stuck her Colt .44 revolver into the terrified faces of three travellers, who between them handed over a total of $428.

Great. The desperados had the swag. However, in their exhilaration, they let the stagecoach go, and it sped back to town with the sizzling news of an old-fashioned stickup—carried out by a female outlaw! It seemed Pearl's disguise hadn't fooled the driver.

Meanwhile, Joe and Pearl wandered aimlessly through the desert. They'd made no plans for escape. They backtracked, sidetracked and got hopelessly lost. Three days later, a local sheriff and his posse tracked them down. As the couple slept by their rain-drenched campfire, the sheriff picked their guns from their holsters and then kicked them both awake. Pearl swore at the sheriff like a crazed banshee and kept up the tirade all the way back to Florence.

Reporters were waiting for her at the jail. They lapped up the story about Pearl wanting to help her poor, ailing mother. And the more Pearl played the uncouth bat out of hell, the more the papers wanted copy on this "wildcat of a woman," and the wilder her performances in front of reporters became. Overnight, she became a celebrity throughout the United States and Canada.

As if she wasn't already in enough trouble, Pearl met another man who got her into even more. Ed Hogan, a convict serving 30 days for being drunk and disorderly, was given the duty of taking Pearl's food to her cell. Ed fell for her big time and tried to persuade her to escape with him. She agreed only when he suggested that, once free, they would set up a band of outlaws together, over which Pearl would reign supreme as their queen. The publicity had gone to Pearl's head.

Two days after Ed's release, he was back at the jail, chiselling an escape hatch through the walls for his beloved. The endeavour took a while because Pearl's bottom was rather large. She eventually squeezed through, and they fled to New Mexico.

The public went wild at this romantic breakout, and the sheriff went ballistic. He caught up with them again and brought them back to Arizona, determined to bring Pearl to justice for the holdup and for her escape.

The courtroom at Joe and Pearl's robbery trial was packed to the rafters. And it wasn't just the public who was full of admiration for the bandit queen. The all-male jury was mesmerized by Pearl's spunky stance and touched by her tales of woe. Most of all, they were reluctant to send a woman to jail. In a highly dramatic wrap-up to the defence's case, a plea was made to set Pearl free so that she could spend time with her gravely ill mother, who only had days to live.

The jury deliberated and, in 10 record-breaking minutes, Pearl was found not guilty. The judge and the sheriff nearly blew a gasket.

But Pearl wasn't off the hook just yet. The judge severely reprimanded the jury for letting her off so lightly because of her sex. He then set up another trial, warning the new jurors to ignore Pearl's gender during their deliberations. Pearl couldn't be tried for the same crime twice, so this time the judge charged her with stealing the stage-coach driver's revolver.

Pearl got her comeuppance the second time around—a five-year sentence—while Joe Boot got 30 years.

But even in jail, Pearl was a celebrity, and reporters wanted to know every single detail about her living conditions, considering she was the only woman in an all-male prison. With all the attention, Pearl soon learned to play the media and the public. Within weeks, she declared she had found God, made grand pronouncements against crime and even took up the cause of the suffragette movement.

The good people of Arizona began to demand her release. It was granted three and a half years into her sentence, but rumour had it that Pearl's liberty ultimately had nothing to do with public pressure. She was allegedly pregnant, and the authorities wanted to avoid a scandal.

Pearl ended her days shrouded in the same mystery that surrounds her early years. She lived in New Mexico for a time with her sister, where they staged a play about Pearl's saga, the "Arizona Bandit." It was a complete failure.

The last verifiable report of Pearl being seen alive came a couple of years after her trial, from Kansas City, Oklahoma, where she was arrested for stealing tinned food. She was granted her freedom as long as she left the state. Pearl was never heard from again.

CHAPTER TEN

Manon Rhéaume
Girl Goalkeeper
(1972–)

*People don't realize the courage that she had to
have to go to NHL level and play and do what she
did. It opened a lot of eyes and it opened a lot of
doors for younger players.*

–Hayley Wickenheiser,
Canadian Women's Olympic Hockey Team

WHEN A SCOUT SHOWED THE NATIONAL HOCKEY LEAGUE
(NHL) team boss a tape of a junior-level hockey
game and asked him what he thought of the goalkeeper, the boss replied, "Okay. The same as all
the others that age. But, he's a bit small." Then the
scout told the boss "he" was a "she." A girl. The boss
was stunned. "Oh my god," he cried, and after he
got over the shock, invited her to an NHL training
camp. For Manon Rhéaume, it was the beginning
of a dream. A real one that came true.

Manon's dream was to play with the big boys.
During her career, the "gorgeous goalie" broke the
ice with a string of firsts in men's professional
hockey. She performed with a smile as big as her

protective padding and a single-minded determination that could fill an Olympic stadium.

She took some seriously hard hits on and off the ice. Blasted by contempt and bruised by sexist sarcasm, Manon picked herself up time after time and stood her ground between the pipes. She came through, not just for herself, but for other women athletes the world over. If she could do it, so can every other woman with a vision.

Manon was born on February 24, 1972, in Lac Beauport, Québec. Her hockey-coach father had her in figure skates by the time she was three. At five, she was playing in goal, stopping the puck for her two brothers, which was the only way they would let her play with them. She loved the game so much, that at seven, she even played with a broken leg in a cast.

The first time she ever played in a rink with other kids, Manon got dressed at home and put her helmet on in the parking lot so that no one else would know she was a girl. It was her dad's idea: let them complain about her gender, after they'd seen how well she could play.

Like thousands of hockey dads, Manon's pushed her to make her game better. He warned her that she wouldn't go far if she whined every time she got hit. "Manon, macramé isn't painful. Choose!" became her father's mantra. She remembered this lesson throughout her career, and from then on she never complained. "I just kept on going. I wanted to be tough," she said in a TV interview.

Manon learned another valuable lesson when one of the hockey dads forced his son into her position as goalie. She settled for playing defence, while her replacement let in goal after goal. Her teammates soon begged her to come back and guard the net. Manon remembers the incident as the first time she learned to face her obstacles and never run away from them.

Manon and her brother Pascal both played on the same PeeWee level men's team. The guys would tease her all the time, telling her to go home and do her laundry. She did nothing of the sort, and in 1984, in front of a crowd of 15,000, Manon became the first girl to play in an international PeeWee tournament.

It was the first time she faced all the pressure of having so much to play for. But she ignored the tension, zoned in on the game and played notably well, even though her team was eliminated in the semifinals. She became an overnight media sensation. One newspaper article predicted she could make it all the way to the NHL—a big prediction for such a little girl. She was only 11 years old.

Handling the media was both a blessing and a necessary evil that Manon had to confront throughout her career. Everyone wanted a piece of her. She was inundated with interview requests, and reporters turned up just to see her play. The hype created intense jealousy from some of her teammates as well as their rivals, spurring the opposition on to an even greater desire to win.

As a teenager, Manon found hockey life to be tough. She fought for every position on every team. She was axed from the top level PeeWee team because the new coach refused to have a girl on his side, although she was clearly better than the other goaltenders. Manon soon realized she was a threat to many fanatical hockey parents. She, a mere girl, was getting in the way of their dreams of an NHL spot for their sons. Besides, hockey in Québec was a religion, and Manon was a sacrilege.

When Manon was 16, her resolve was finally tested to its limits. This was the age when players moved up to Bantam level, and all her teammates, in fact every single player and goalie in Québec, were invited to the Triple A tryouts. Except Manon.

After that, she couldn't find a position on any team, not even at the lower level she had been playing on. All her frustration came to a head during a non-competition game in Bernière St. Nicholas. Manon became aware that the guys were intentionally shooting high. For a while she kept jumping to avoid being hit in the face. It was obvious they were really trying to hurt her, so she came out of the net to attack. Instead of feeling sorry for herself, she went into a rage. This was the

first and last time Manon ever "lost it" on the ice.
When the game was over, she was more hurt on
the inside than on the outside—so much so that
she questioned whether she would ever play
hockey at a higher level, or even if she wanted to.

A break from hockey for a full year became
a cooling-off period. Manon enrolled in college to
take a degree in humanities but didn't complete
it. She met a girl there who played in the women's
hockey league, and Manon decided if she couldn't
play with the guys, she would play with the girls.

Within weeks, Manon's confidence was back
and overflowing. Her Sherbrooke team went all
the way to the Canadian Women's Finals, and she
scored the winning goal. Her luck began to turn.
Gaston Drapeau, the coach for Québec's Les
Draveurs, saw the game and invited Manon to
practise with the men's team. She was ecstatic.
This was a Junior Major team, the highest level
before turning pro.

Determination got Manon on the team, but only
as the third- or fourth-string goaltender. As luck
would have it, she was given a big break due to
another goalie's injury and played her first junior
major hockey game—the first woman ever to do so,
and the second of Manon's long list of records. The
team lost, but Manon made some memorable saves.

She received a standing ovation, as well as
a massive gash on her eye for her trouble, caused
by a shot so hard it broke her helmet. The blood

kept pouring down her face but she wouldn't pull out of the game. Her father was right; macramé was off the menu for Manon.

The media scrum in the dressing room afterwards was vindication for all the skeptics who believed she was just a girl and couldn't physically cut it. Her eye injury was proof that she shouldn't be playing hockey. But Manon took the onslaught with aplomb. Under the barrage of lights and condescending questions, she calmly announced she was just going to take every day as it came and see whether her fitness would hold up as well as her dream.

For the first time in years Manon was riding high. On top of the eye-gashing game, she had a gold medal win with Team Canada in the Women's World Championships in 1992. In the final against archrivals the U.S., she scored a shutout that led to an 8–0 victory for her team. Her luck had finally turned, and her perseverance was paying off.

Someone must have been watching over Manon, because a scout sent a tape of the game where she gashed her eye to Tampa Bay Lightning boss, Phil Esposito. Esposito was intrigued—and smart—a girl on the team could be a great marketing gimmick. He invited her for a fortnight to his upcoming NHL training camp, making sure to warn the press and his stupefied coaching staff.

The Tampa Bay Lightning was the newest team in the NHL. The team, located in an unlikely hockey town in sunny Florida, needed all the publicity it could get. The day Manon arrived at camp, all of the major U.S. networks turned up. Manon agreed to play the media if doing it paid her for playing the game she loved.

Manon's first game in training camp was another a superb shutout—no goal scored against her in 15 attempts. She'd won some respect. "You really shut them up. They're going to take you seriously from now on," said one player. A woman had never taken part in an NHL training camp before, and Manon ended it with the third-best goals against average.

But there was no time to rest. After the camp came the exhibition matches. On the team bus going to the game against the St. Louis Blues, everyone, including Manon, was wondering if they would have a job the next day.

That day was September 23, 1992. Twenty-year-old Manon watched the first period and had time to assess the opponents and the fact that she was about to become the first woman to play in an NHL game. She put aside the doubts and the victimization she'd experienced in getting there—the coach had refused to speak to her throughout the camp, and most of the players didn't want a girl on their side, period. But this was the moment she'd been waiting to prove to everyone all her life.

The crowd stood and cheered as she took to the ice for the second period. She stopped the first shot. And the second. And a few more before the puck ricocheted off her pads into the back of the net. She let in a second goal, but not even the best goalie in the league could have saved it. It wasn't a bad performance by any standards. "There wasn't a woman in the house that night that wasn't cheering her brains out for her [Manon]," said Esposito.

Manon was pleased, though the team lost 6–4. Even the coach smiled at her at last, and Esposito too. At the press conference later, considering how far she had come, the sacrifices she'd made, and the respect she'd gleaned from previously skeptical teammates, one reporter was macho enough to ask, "Did you break a fingernail?" Manon's blood boiled, and she demanded of him, "Would you ask that question to any other goalkeeper?"

Manon had won the hearts of thousands but had angered just as many who still thought she had no place in men's sports, so they dismissed her one and only NHL period in goal as a freak sideshow and publicity stunt. For Manon it was a dream come true, so even if Esposito was using her, she was okay with it. "I have a chance to do higher than I can and I have the chance to try," Manon commented in her still rather broken English.

Esposito didn't sign her up for the NHL but sent her to the Atlanta Knights, a farm team for Tampa Bay. For a woman, this was an incredible feat and another first—a three-year men's pro-hockey contract. Now she had to push her physical fitness to the limit, practising every day instead of the twice-a-week workouts she was used to.

But at the press conference to announce the news, cynical journalists reverted to cheap degradation rather than admit that a woman had just broken down some major testosterone barriers. One journalist had the gall to ask Manon how her game was affected when she has her period. She told him that was when she played her best. Other questions were designed to belittle her, such as why had she refused a $75,000 offer from *Playboy* for a nude picture deal. Manon knew she had to become as skillful at deflecting media put-downs as she was at deflecting the puck.

Atlanta was a lonely time for Manon, but a busy one too. Not only did she practise more than every other player, but she also wrote her autobiography, *Manon: Alone in Front of the Net*, improved her English and did so much promotion she got a stomach ulcer from the stress.

She also wasn't played much—just one five-minute stint in an early game of the season, and one more at the end. She was sitting it out on the benches and not doing what she loved most—playing goal. Eventually, Esposito agreed to her request to play for a lower level team and to do far less promotion.

That Manon was a miracle marketing tool for hockey is indisputable. She was talented, beautiful and sexy, and some commentators attributed the buzz around her as a major contributing factor to having women's hockey included in the Olympics. For the first time, the 1998 Olympic Games in Nagano, Japan, would include women's hockey. Manon now had her sights on yet another dream.

In the meantime, Manon spent the next few years moving from team to team in the East and West Coast Leagues in the U.S. She remembers most players at this time treating her kindly because she'd broken down so many barriers, always given a 100 percent and never complained.

With every new team, arrangements were made for her to change in the referee's room or some other safety zone—something Manon had learned from Phil Esposito, who admitted in his memoirs that he had sneaked a peek at Manon's bare derriere.

In 1996 Manon also started to play professional roller hockey, which is about as different from ice hockey as racquetball is from tennis—much faster and higher scoring. She was the first woman to win a game in the pro-men's league. And it was while playing roller hockey that Manon had her first serious relationship, with Gerry St. Cyr, a former NHL hockey player who switched to pro-roller hockey and became the league's top player. They didn't even like each other at first but eventually married in 1998.

Manon played a pivotal role in defending Team Canada's gold medal at the World Championships, winning it a second time at Lake Placid, New York, in 1994, and for the second time in a row she won the accolade of Most Valuable Player of the tournament. And in pro-hockey, all the blood, sweat and tears paid off. Manon had her best-ever year in pro-hockey in 1997. She played 11 games and had the best goalie average on her team, the Reno Renegades. Now she was looking forward to being part of the Olympic team, which was just a year away.

So when the blow came, it hit her like a 10-ton truth truck. Manon was devastated to discover that coach Shannon Miller cut her from the Canadian women's Olympic team. Miller claimed the two other goalies played more consistently. Manon couldn't believe it. Visibly shaken, she nearly broke down in front of the cameras.

Somehow, over the next year, for the sake of a dream, Manon once again dug out every ounce of determination she possessed. She practised until she couldn't walk and blocked pucks until she was blue. She would make the team if it killed her.

Once again her grit and her guts were rewarded. Manon made the team that went to Nagano in 1998. And the team made the final. And history. Manon started off in goal for the first-ever Canadian Women's Olympic Hockey Team, and she played like an angel sent from heaven, which couldn't be said of the rest of the team, according to the critics. Team Canada eventually lost to its U.S. archrivals, but commentators said that throughout the game Manon had been "standing on her head for Canada. She held the Canadians in the game."

In 1999 Manon took on a whole new challenge with the birth of her son Dylan. A year later she retired from the Women's National Hockey League.

These days Manon spends her time inspiring more and more girls to take advantage of the trail she has blazed for them. She and husband Gerry host training camps for girls and organize tournaments in the hopes that at least one of them, one day, will play professional hockey.

Manon is even making the shoe fit better, designing a hockey skate specially for girls that has a higher instep and more ankle support.

But most importantly, Manon reminds her protégés every day that they shouldn't fear playing sports against boys. "Do what you want to do," she tells them. "If someone tries to stop you, just try harder." And what better inspiration for the next generation of "hockeyeuses" than to have their mentor be the woman who actually lived the example she champions.

CHAPTER ELEVEN

Tana Dineen
Turncoat Psychologist
(1948–)

I couldn't maintain my integrity in a profession that is almost devoid of integrity. This book is my apology for decades of biting my lip about the pernicious effects psychologists are having on individuals and society.

–Tana Dineen

IT TOOK HER 30 YEARS OF HANDS-ON EXPERIENCE AS A CLINICAL psychologist for Tana to load up her guns. Then she aimed and emptied a machine-gun's worth of criticism into her own profession.

The bullet was the book *Manufacturing Victims: What the Psychology Industry is Doing to People* (1996), an unflinching critique of the psychology "industry" that, in Dineen's opinion, creates a host of artificial victims and a poor-me mentality across society as a whole.

But she reserves her biggest bullets for the army of therapists who charge a fortune to "heal" people of all sorts of imaginary imbalances, neuroses, syndromes and the so-called treatments they prescribe that have no basis in scientific fact.

"Over the years, I have seen my profession, which used to ask fascinating and important questions, simply provide answers without bothering to verify whether there is any scientific basis to those answers," Dineen said.

As a case in point, Dineen cites grief counselling, which was prescribed for a whole nation it seems after the 9/11 terrorist attacks. But there have never been any studies on whether grief counselling actually works. In her book, Dineen suggests that a hug from a friendly neighbour is just as effective and a lot cheaper.

Dineen's criticism does not denounce psychology in its totality. She praises the value of properly conducted scientific research. But she is really after the charlatans who give the profession a bad name. She is also careful to differentiate between real victims (of war, torture or sexual assault) and the "manufactured" ones created by notions such as the now debunked "recovered memory syndrome."

Ever since getting her PhD in 1975 from the University of Saskatchewan and then becoming a licensed psychologist in 1977, Dineen has specialized in research on how the personal beliefs of psychologists and other mental health "experts" affect the treatment of their patients.

Her research found that the imposition of those beliefs has become widespread today, so much so that she tours the world warning people that the current practice of psychology is unethical because the "profession" is creating a society of victims.

Dineen's research also supports her theory that women are the most gullible. They are most prone to believe the utopian promises made by the "professionals" of an over-sentimentalized ideal of society, and most prone to believing there is something wrong with them if they don't strive for that ideal and achieve it. Dineen devotes pages and pages of her book to berating the type of pop psychology spouted in TV talk shows, self-help books and women's magazines, because it gives respectable psychology a bad name.

Dineen's colleagues cried foul at these accusations, presumably because they had the most to lose. She was nicknamed the "Renegade Psychologist" by her peers in Canada. Today Dineen is invited all over the world to set the psychological world to rights. She talks to judges, lawyers, police officers, ethicists, criminologists and philosophers about what's wrong—with other psychologists.

Dineen's views may annoy her colleagues, but her views are so well respected by the medical establishment that she was appointed as the first (and, to date, the only) non-medical treatment director of a large Canadian psychiatric hospital.

For the future, Dr. Dineen prescribes some controversial remedies for an "industry" that has gone so crazy it creates nutcases out of normal people. One of her remedies is to eradicate the licensing of psychologists because it gives them legally sanctioned power and unjustified scientific kudos. Without licensing, therapists would be on the same footing as astrologers and psychics. Her other remedies include getting rid of insurance coverage for psychological services and stopping the public funding of victim support groups, court-ordered treatment programs, compensation for psychological stress and damage, paid stress leave and mandatory stress debriefing for victims of trauma. She also wants to stop psychologists from appearing as expert witnesses in court because they can fool the judge and jury into thinking that their testimony is based on scientific research when it isn't. Her last remedy is to punish "junk therapy" by allowing "patients" to launch lawsuits.

Dineen has a much simpler cure that works for everyone. And all victims disappear to boot. "If we move beyond blaming, whether the object of blame be a person, a country, or an ideology, we can assume responsibility for our lives and for the state of the world," she states.

Now that's radical.

CHAPTER TWELVE

Klondike Kate
Dance-Hall Queen of the Yukon
(1876–1957)

It wasn't that I was bad. I was just imaginative and full of life and the excitement of living.

–Kitty Rockwell

THERE WERE TWO KLONDIKE KATES. KITTY GOT UP TO NO good, while Kathryn was a do-gooder.

Kitty was a sassy dance-hall girl who got rich by batting her beautiful eyelashes at lonely Yukon prospectors while relieving them of rather large numbers of gold nuggets.

This Klondike Kate is not to be confused with Kathryn Ryan who was born in 1869 and became the first female member of the North-West Mounted Police, the first female gold inspector, a jail keeper, restaurateur, nurse and respectable citizen involved in business and political affairs.

The two Kates did meet eventually. One of them served a month-long sentence for prostitution. The other one locked her up. This story is about the Kitty who spent time behind bars.

❦

Kathleen "Kitty" Eloisa Rockwell was born in Kansas City in 1876. Her ma divorced her pa when Kitty was five and then remarried the super-rich and pompous Judge Frank Bettis of Spokane, Washington. Frank adored Kitty, and mother and daughter lived a life of luxury and high social standing.

The young Kitty learned to speak her mind as fearlessly as her stepfather. She had the ways of a gypsy, always on the go, running and dancing, doing the unexpected. Once, she opened up the family home to all and sundry who lost their homes when a fire destroyed the town. She caused an uproar among proper society by playing hooky from school, flirting outrageously with the boys and dancing uncontrollably whenever she heard music.

Kitty was sent to a convent to calm her down. It didn't work. She became even wilder after her stepfather's death, when she was sent by boat to relatives in Valpariso, Chile. She learned to flirt with all the sailors during the 78-day voyage, and when she arrived—as the only unmarried American girl in town—she fell in and out of love with young gentlemen who gave her diamond rings, which she accepted with empty promises. When Kitty's mother heard of these antics, she sent for her daughter immediately.

Kitty and her mother, Martha, later settled in New York during the "naughty nineties"—the

world was loosening up, there was music everywhere, and Kitty took to the footlights as a chorus
girl. Her mother was outraged. But they needed
Kitty's salary. Martha chaperoned her daughter
everywhere to keep her in check, but when Kitty
got away from her mother's clutches while on tour
and had her first taste of freedom, she wasn't going
to give it up.

Martha never knew that singing and dancing
was only part of a chorus girl's job description. Ply-
ing men with drinks and getting a commission for
the booze she sold was the lucrative part. The well-
brought-up Miss Rockwell despaired at first, but
she quickly learned the tricks of the trade. Then an
offer came to go north and entertain the rush of
gold diggers infected with get-rich-quick fever up
in the Yukon.

It was a perilous journey north for Kitty, until
she reached her bedroom above the dance hall of
the Savoy Theatre in Dawson, the City of Gold.
Within weeks she was top bill, setting the town
alight, as well as her own hair, in her famous
"flame dance." Costumed with lighted candles on
her head, Kitty swirled miles and miles of red fab-
ric around the stage like torches, singing her heart
out.

The gold miners were dazzled, and they show-
ered her with appreciative gold nuggets. She was
soon making more money than they were—some
nights she landed $500 in commission for selling

alcohol and listening to the miners' sob stories: failed grubstakes, families back home that they missed terribly. Kitty listened, danced and got them drunk.

She was a raven-haired beauty who soon got over any qualms about accepting endless gifts from wealthy big shots. She had a devil-may-care sparkle that miners loved and society despised. Kitty always claimed to be a high-class entertainer, yet she thrived in the cabaret halls, "sacrificing professional standards for the sake of money and excitement," claimed her biographer, Ellis Lucia.

Nevertheless, Kitty was idolized as the "Queen of the Yukon." Many of the miners fondly remembered her sincerity, generous heart and constant willingness to help others in trouble, even lending them money when their luck turned sour.

But these acts of charity did nothing to endear her to the "respectable" women of the town, the wives of religious men and government administrators. To them, there was no difference between dance-hall girls like Kitty and the devil-ridden harlots of "Lousetown," where the prostitutes lived. Indeed, the line was a thin one, and Kitty later admitted in her memoirs that, "Sometimes a girl blended now and then. I'm not trying to put over the idea that we were vestal virgins. Far from it. We fell head over heels in love, and we made mistakes."

In her old age, Kitty tried to clean up her image, claiming she never sold herself, because she was saving herself for the "right man." But the truth was that Kitty was arrested for prostitution and served a month-long sentence in 1902. Her jailor was the other Klondike Kate, Kathryn Ryan.

Eventually, the right man did come along. Or so it seemed at the time. He was a good-looking Greek bartender named Alexander Pantages. In contrast to the unkempt "sourdoughs" (the name given to those who'd spent at least one winter mining for gold), Alex was a dapper, well-dressed, barrel-chested hunk of a man. Kitty fell for him instantly, and never fell out of love, despite a roller-coaster affair of broken dreams, shattered promises, abuse and obsession.

The other sourdoughs couldn't see what Kitty saw in Alex, but for a while the couple made a great team, both earning a fortune working the bars and clubs. When Alex lost his job, Kitty kept him in the expensive style to which he'd grown accustomed, and he claimed her as his girl.

In 1901, Kitty "acquired" a child. Until her dying day, Kitty claimed she cared for the boy because his mother died of tuberculosis and his father ran off. She kept him in Dawson for three years "until he became as dear to me as if he had been my own," but sent him away to keep him safe from the tawdry world of dance halls. Kitty paid for the boy's upkeep for years, leading some to claim that when she settled years later in the back-of-beyond town of Bend, Oregon, the only reason she did so

was to be close to her "son," who never knew her
real identity.

Alex and Kitty talked of marriage, but he kept
putting it off. Kitty's mother was outraged when
she discovered the two were living together. But
it was normal behaviour for couples to keep each
other warm during the long cold nights of a Yukon
winter, with or without a marriage licence. Victorian America was disgusted, and Kitty lived with
a sullied reputation for the rest of her life.

Alex used Kitty's money, and together they
went into partnership as owners of the Orpheum
Theatre. It soon became the most popular place in
town, eventually grossing over $8000 a day—
a shining example of Alex's genius sensitivity to
how people wanted to be entertained and his ability to provide it. Kitty headlined, and they pulled
in the best entertainers from across the country. It
wasn't all golden, however. The theatre burned
down three times and had to be rebuilt each time.

Meanwhile, the gold strikes were running out,
and it was clear that Dawson's heyday was over.
The couple criss-crossed the U.S. trying to find
a site for a new theatre, posing as husband and
wife to relatives and friends. Alex returned to
Dawson alone, persuading Kitty to try to make
some cash in Texas, where oil was now the new
gold. They agreed that she'd send him the money
she made, for investment in what Kitty believed
was their *joint* enterprise.

Alex wrote her love letters from the Yukon, until one day a letter came that stabbed Kitty right through the heart. Not only had Alex spent her cash and bought a new theatre without her, but he also had married a young violin player. Kitty was devastated, stunned and incredulous, and she took up drinking. The only thing that pulled her out of a pit of despair was bitterness. She filed a $25,000 breach-of-promise suit against her ex-lover.

The papers had a field day. The front page of the *Seattle Daily Times* read, "Uses her money, then jilts the girl"—surprisingly sympathetic to a woman of Kitty's reputation, but Alex wasn't exactly considered a paragon of virtue either. The torrid details of their affair and his betrayal hooked readers for weeks. Kitty claimed that Alex used her grubstake to build a lucrative business, all the while promising to marry her.

Alex at first denied even knowing Kitty. But he then admitted she was "an acquaintance," despite evidence of hotel bills from across the country in the name of "Mr. and Mrs. Pantages." The sourdoughs up North, disgusted at how he'd treated Kitty, swore Pantages was now their enemy for life.

The case dragged on, and eventually Kitty lost heart, which was already broken anyway. She settled out of court for a paltry $5000. As far as the public was concerned, Kitty was a low-life, trying to squeeze money out of a rich man by any means necessary. Kitty never forgave or forgot Alex, and

years later they met again in court, for what many
people claim was her revenge.

In the meantime, she was a vaudeville girl with
no money. Kitty hooked up with various theatre
men and toured the country performing. Most of
the time she was fending off nervous breakdowns,
just scraping by and scraping her knees in ever-
more dangerous acts, until one day she fell so
badly, she never danced again.

Then Kitty went wild, literally. She bought
a horse and wandered around Oregon until she
found a tiny plot of land in a town called Bend.
She had a small amount of money, a few diamonds
and gold nuggets, as well as a trunk full of memories and stage clothes.

The people of Bend didn't know what to make
of this curious "homesteader" who planted vegeta-
bles in lacy bloomers and stage-made corsets.
Tongues started wagging when the men of the
town stopped by to fix this or that, brought by
a cut of venison or asked her out on a date. The suit-
ors often sat in Kitty's ramshackle hut, desperately
trying to outstay each other to extract a promise
from her for something more.

Kitty loved the gossip and all the attention.
Then, she really gave the town something to talk
about when she rode off into the sunset to marry
a handsome devil called Floyd Warner, who was
19 years her junior. Folks thought she only married him for his father's ranch, and while Floyd

was away working, she ran around the country and around town, leaving behind her a wake of stories about other men with whom she had danced the night away.

Instead of fighting with Kitty over it, Floyd left to fight World War I in Europe, and Kitty went to work in town. When he returned, they fought for a year because she refused to play the dutiful wife, until she eventually filed for divorce, claiming Floyd had beaten her.

When the couple split, Kitty was broke again. She went begging to ex-lover Alex Pantages, who now lived in Los Angeles, the millionaire owner of a theatre empire. Alex only agreed to see her for fear she would fabricate some sort of scandal or blackmail if he didn't. He handed Kitty the $6 in his wallet, turned away and closed the door behind him. She cried all the way back to the train station and all the way back on the journey home to Bend.

Kitty had lived her whole life surrounded by men, addicted to the attention she craved from them. She spent the next few years as the "mama" of the Bend Fire Department, taking care of her "boys" and making sure there was a pot of hot coffee on the stove for them after every fire. The men loved her and called her "Aunt Kate," but tongues wagged again about what they got up to.

"Aunt Kate was sure darn good to the fire depart-ment. We never cared what folks said about her, or what she might have been," said one fireman.

But for most of society in Bend, Kitty was a "har-lot," and once a harlot always a harlot.

Despite her good works, such as nursing the sick during the Spanish flu epidemic in 1918, Kitty couldn't shake off her past, and she became known as "our destitute prostitute" when she begged food scraps for a soup kitchen during the Depression.

She was seen as a busybody who fought with her neighbours, was blunt and outspoken, dressed like a chorus girl and always looked for publicity. The local newspaper, the *Bulletin*, eventually banned the printing of any more stories about her. But Kitty held her head up high during the '20s and '30s, whether people liked her or not.

As Kitty scraped by, Alex Pantages built high— the biggest empire of theatres ever known across the United States. He screened movies as well as vaudeville acts and theatre. Future stars had their careers launched in his theatres, and Alex never went by an agent's word; he insisted on audition-ing every performer himself.

However, he probably wished he'd never set eyes on a 17-year-old dancer by the name of Eunice Pringle. In 1929 she ran out of his office, screaming that Pantages molested her during an audition. Alex maintained it was a frame-up to extort some of the $24 million he'd just made selling his theatres to RKO (Radio-Keith-Orpheum), a major motion picture company.

Some historians suggest that the frame-up was actually Kitty's idea to get revenge on her former lover. Others say it started out as a prank by the miners who never forgave Alex for the way he'd treated Kitty. The sourdoughs would do anything for their beloved Queen of the Yukon, and some believe the miners took seriously a throw-away comment Kitty made about wanting to exact revenge on Alex, so they set him up.

It was up to the courts to decide the truth. Kitty was subpoenaed, and she attended the trial every day. She even met Alex once in the corridor and burst into tears. It appeared she was still in love with him. Again the newspapers had a field day, digging up the details of the couple's old affair and Alex's betrayal. While Kitty revelled in being the subject of endless articles that gave her a chance to relive her glory days, she always maintained she never plotted against the theatre man for revenge.

Kitty was never actually called as a character witness, so we'll never know what her testimony might have been, but Pantages was found guilty without it. He faced two more trials before he was finally acquitted in 1936. The court ruled that Eunice had been lying in a plot designed by her manager to extort Pantages' money.

Pantages never recovered from the scandal. He died suddenly a few months after the final verdict. But his downfall caused Kitty's star to rise over the next few years. She became a celebrity and a legend during the trial and then became the toast of the town, giving speech after speech and becoming the subject of media interviews. Kitty was in her element.

Far away, back in the Yukon, Johnny Matson, known as the "Silent Swede," who had first set eyes on Kitty 30 years earlier, read an article about her. Johnny wrote Kitty a letter saying, "I have always been in love with you, Katie...You have had lots of hardships. I would like to have the right to take care of you as my wife."

Thus started a romance in 1931 that became the stuff of legend. But by all accounts, the marriage between Kitty and Johnny was a bizarre affair. After their wedding in 1933, the couple communicated only by letter for years, dependent on whether the snow and ice allowed Johnny to travel the 97 kilometres from his grubstake to the post office.

Kitty visited Johnny once a year. They'd spend a weekend in a hotel in Dawson, and she'd leave again. Matson kept his promise and looked after Kitty financially, but she kept putting off her promise to move back to the Yukon to live with him, and he never made the trip to Bend. Kitty's critics speculated that she was merely up to her old tricks of using her body to get money from a man. The marriage continued in this way until the spring of 1946 when Johnny's letters stopped. After a long search, his body was found 48 kilometres from his home. He had taken shelter from a storm in a shack, but the wolves had got to him.

Not one for grieving, two years later, at the tender age of 71, Kitty again tied the knot with her long-time friend from Bend, Bill Van Duren. When the judge asked Bill why he requested the three-day waiver normally required before a marriage licence could be granted, Bill replied, "Time is of the essence." Bill was also 71. The judge must have sympathized with their plight—the marriage went ahead immediately.

The couple had nine good years living together in a place called Sweet Home until Kitty died in her sleep in February 1957 at the age of 81.

Some said Kitty Rockwell was "the biggest fake of all time." Others claimed "she was the kindest person I ever knew." Love her or hate her, she spent a lifetime rocking the boat and pushing the boundaries. *Time* and *Newsweek* reported her passing as the end of an era, and Kitty would have smiled to know that the ban imposed at Bend's *Bulletin* newspaper was lifted for one final mention: "Her story is one that will grow as memories of Alaska's gold rush fade into distant history."

CHAPTER THIRTEEN

Anne Clare Cools
Spiky Senator
(1943–)

The Senator from Toronto is earning a reputation for "poking a sharp stick in the eye" of the feminists who elected her.

–Margaret Wente, *Globe and Mail*, March 1, 1997

ANNE COOLS WAS THE DARLING OF THE FEMINIST MOVEMENT for her untiring commitment to highlighting the plight of battered women. She walked her talk and pioneered practical and legal ways to help them. As an advocate for the cause, in the 1970s Cools braved the derision of those who preferred to brush the issues of equality, and domestic violence in particular, under the carpet.

But then she turned. First, in the name of upholding family values, Cools championed the cause of fathers and nearly torpedoed legislation that would give mothers more rights than fathers after divorce. And then, in 2004, the woman who made her career as a Liberal politician, and was appointed as a Liberal to the Senate by the Liberal government of Prime Minister Pierre Trudeau, defected to the Conservatives, because she believed the concept of "family" was safer in their hands than the Liberals'.

Anne was born in Barbados in 1943 and came to Canada when she was 13. Her parents taught her two major lessons when she was growing up: society owes no one anything, and everyone has a responsibility to contribute to society.

Anne got a Bachelor of Arts degree from McGill University in Montréal. She had her first anti-authoritarian brush with the law in the 1960s when, as a young student activist, she was sentenced to four months in prison for her involvement in the Sir George Williams University computer riot. It was the largest student riot in Canadian history, ignited by the university's alleged mishandling of racist allegations against one of its professors.

On her release, Anne embarked upon a life of innovation, leading the way in creating social services for battered women. In 1974 she set up the first women's shelter in Canada—Women in Transition—in Toronto, and served as its executive director. Her good works in this arena were rewarded in 1984 when Anne became the first black person appointed to the Senate. It was a popular move and a great score for the political PR team at the time. Women's groups expected Anne to represent them.

But the first signs of trouble, as far as the women's lib movement was concerned, came in 1995 when Senator Cools uttered some sharp words—on International Women's Day of all days—about the issue of child abuse. "Behind every abusing husband is an abusing mother," she said. Women's groups across the country were apoplectic at her suggestion that violent sons were the product of abusive mothers. Armies of experts were brought in on the other side of the battle lines to claim that Cools was totally and utterly wrong, and the liberal press openly expressed concerns about the senator's sanity.

Since then, studies have shown that Cools was partly right. Abusers are much more likely to have been abused themselves, and mothers are more likely than fathers to be the perpetrators because mothers spend more time with the children. But as commentators point out, this doesn't make all men innocent, nor does it make all women victimizers.

The senator's views, however, punched holes in the prevailing feminist ideology that all men are bullies and all women their victims. The radicals claimed that Cools was selling out. Anne hit back against charges that she had become a renegade anti-feminist. She claimed it wasn't she who had changed but the feminist movement itself. "The radicals have hijacked the agenda," she said in her defence. "They see men as evil and will stop at nothing to ensure the superiority of women."

Comments like these were jumped on by fanatical men's rights groups and appropriated as part of a new "equalizing gender gospel" by politicians, predominantly white males, in the Reform party.

For many activists, there's nothing worse than a turncoat. So it was a bitter pill for them to swallow when Anne bit the hand that had given her a political platform in the first place.

When Justice Minister Allan Rock introduced legislation in 1997 to change child-support provisions after couples divorce, Cools opposed it as another example of anti-male legislation. She thought it would force fathers to pay huge chunks of cash to mothers, regardless of what mothers earned, and yet still not guarantee a father's access to his children. The Liberals only had a majority of one in the Senate at the time, so her potential defection was seen as a harsh betrayal. Cools eventually voted for the bill, but not before she forced through some amendments.

Cools' position as a Liberal was becoming untenable, but she made no apologies, and her views became ever-more vociferous. In a speech to the International Fatherhood Conference in Washington, DC, in 2002, Cools declared, "Misguided policies in social welfare law, in family law, in divorce law, in child welfare law, in abortion law have resulted in national problems, in our crises of father-alienation and fatherlessness."

A shocked media began to describe Ms. Anne Cools in their reports as a renegade, rebel and an anti-feminist maverick. In private and off the record, Liberal party operatives call her loopy, a bit of a fruitcake and a loose cannon.

Senator Cools turned her back on the Liberals in 2004. Laurie Arron, the political coordinator for Canadians for Equal Marriage, summed up the feelings of many activists when Cools took up her Conservative seat in the Senate. "She has opposed equality for gay and lesbian people at every turn. She will, I'm sure, feel right at home in the new Conservative Party."

CHAPTER FOURTEEN

Alanis Obomsawin
First Nations Filmmaker
(1932–)

A pioneering artist, singer, educator, community activist, Member [now Officer] *of the Order of Canada, Obomsawin is to her legion of admirers a legend in her own time.*

–Adrian Harewood, *Take One* magazine

ALANIS OBOMSAWIN'S NAME MEANS "PATHFINDER." SHE had to beat down her own path, and many doors in the process, to become Canada's most renowned First Nations documentary filmmaker. Her career and life are marked with beauty, elegance and burning passion.

Some say her films revolutionized Aboriginal art, others say they are excessively subjective and one-sided—but everyone on both sides of the fence recognizes that Alanis is a woman with a fire in her heart. Her mission is to castigate the government for brutality and immorality against her people. Her weapon of choice? A camera.

Obomsawin has stated that her role is "to make sure that our people are heard! I want to expose the injustices. I look for social changes. [My role] is to make sure that these films, these documents, are used in the educational system."

Alanis refuses to separate her roles as filmmaker, activist and community leader. The combination has proven formidable and has instigated change, not only in legislation but also in the hearts and minds of Canadians—her tireless efforts helped transform vehemently negative stereotypes against Native people into understanding.

Alanis' first big struggle came when she was six months old. It was for her life. She had fallen into a coma, and no one knew why. The little girl's situation looked hopeless, and expectations for her recovery began to fade, when a revered aunt suddenly appeared and took the baby away to care for her. "Nobody knows what she did to me, but I survived," Alanis explains in a *Cinema Canada* article.

A wonderful next few years made up for young Alanis' terrible start in life. She is a member of the Abenaki nation, born in New Hampshire in 1932, but she grew up on the Odanak reserve northeast of Montréal. Her father was a hunting and fishing guide, her mother a healer of traditional Native medicine. Alanis was surrounded by a loving brood of older women who told her age-old stories and sang time-honoured songs. By the time she was nine, Alanis held a deep reverence and love for her culture. But comfort was soon ripped from under her feet.

Her family moved to Trois-Riviéres, Québec. It was only 50 kilometres away but, for Alanis, it might as well have been another planet—no one spoke English, only French, and she and her family were the only Natives in town. Alanis became the target of racism and abuse, and suffered almost daily at the hands of her schoolmates who beat her up and spit racist names at her. "'Dirty Indian,' stuff like that," Alanis remembers in a *Calgary Herald* article.

Alanis clearly recalls one teacher who twisted her fingernails into the girl's arm, calling her a "savage"—an image perpetuated in the school's chauvinistic history books. Experiences like this fuelled the older Alanis' pledge to change the education system.

The abuse, however, didn't dint Alanis' or her parents' stoicism, nor their spiritual beliefs and cultural traditions. There wasn't a hint of retaliation; indeed, her parents often treated neighbours for illnesses with their traditional medicines.

Instead of turning inward with self-loathing as many victims of racism tend to do, Alanis became stronger, refusing to believe the limitations that others set for her and all Native people. "I knew that there was a lot of wrong there. Every time I tried to do something, they would tell me, 'Oh you can't do this, you're an Indian!' The more they said that to me, the more I said, 'Well, I am going to do

that anyway.' I was just a fighter. I just wanted
to make changes," she stated in an interview for
Take One.

But tragedy struck again. This time, Alanis
emerged from it doggedly determined and self-
reliant. Her father, who had lived with tuberculosis
for years, finally succumbed to the disease. Weeks
later, she took control of her own life. "When I was
12, my father died. I decided I wasn't going to get
beat up at school every day by the other girls in
the classroom. It was just a decision—just like that
I said, 'no more.' And that's all there was to it. It
stopped the next day."

The lesson the teenage Alanis learned, to take
responsibility for her own destiny and take pride in
her heritage, developed into an almost transcen-
dent goal—to tell the stories of her people. As she
told *Windspeaker* magazine, "That was my fight
from the very beginning, to fight for changes in
the educational system concerning our people, and
I wanted to see our history being taught and to try
and do our own programs and get it in there as
part of the curriculum."

But before she embarked on that crusade, she
spent a little time exploring her future. As a dark-
haired beauty with a natural elegance, Alanis
worked as a model in Florida. She initially went
there to improve her English and did this by reading Canada's *Indian Act*—unlikely bedtime reading
for most people—but Alanis was determined to

understand the workings of a law that had so afflicted her people. In the late '50s she settled in Montréal, where she still lives, in a house she has now spent more than half her life.

While the '60s got into full swing and radicals became hip, Alanis hung out with a circle of writers and artists that included the young Leonard Cohen. This clique of cultured intellectuals and songwriters inspired Alanis to become a singer.

Very soon, armed with all the songs and stories she had translated from her childhood, Alanis set out on the road to elevate and educate the young. Her mission was to instill self-esteem in Native children and pride in their oral histories. She made her professional debut on stage in New York in 1960, and since then has played everywhere from schools to prisons, folk festivals to museums.

Alanis' work caught the attention of the CBC (Canadian Broadcasting Corporation), which profiled Alanis as the activist chanteuse in the 1965 documentary *Telescope*. The program pricked up the ears of the National Film Board (NFB), who asked Obomsawin to be an advisor on a film about Aboriginal people. She agreed, motivated by her budding interest in film and its potential to bring personal stories to a mass audience. Soon Alanis was making her own films. Her first film, *Christmas at Moose Factory* (1971), was a collection of children's crayon drawings showing different scenes of everyday life around the shores of James Bay.

And thus began a lifelong relationship with the NFB. Alanis today is one of only three staff directors at the institute where she has made over 16 films, many of them award-winning, and most of them so provocative they hit at the very core of the nation's cultural tensions.

But it isn't just Alanis' willpower that got her through racial barriers—it is her qualities as a human being. She is a woman of dignity and grace, who is humble without affectation, mischievous and funny, yet fearsome when challenged. Her life force comes from the love and compassion she holds for the ignored and the desperate.

John Grierson, the NFB's founder, met Alanis in the early '70s and was spellbound by her poise and talent. She was exactly the sort of filmmaker the NFB was established to support. She, in turn, was captivated by Grierson's belief in the liberating power of film, in particular that poor and ordinary people should be able to see positive and sympathetic images of themselves on screen.

To get these "positive images" of her people made, Alanis pounded on doors to raise cash—and she didn't take no for an answer. The NFB and Department of Indian Affairs turned down funding for her second film, *Mother of Many Children* (1977), because its subject matter—the role of the matriarch in Aboriginal culture—was not of interest. She then thumped on the Secretary of State's door in Ottawa instead and got the money. He told her later that it was the best film they had funded so far.

For the next 15 years, Alanis' films were revolutionary in the sense that, at last, an Aboriginal was making them. Her films were groundbreaking because her documentaries were positively steeped in appreciation of her ancestry. They also were made with the permission and participation of Aboriginals, who for so long were either ignored as movie subjects or filmed without their consent and turned into objects—"savages" mostly—who took up arms in the face of "civilizing forces," a.k.a. the white man. Or, in the few positive cinematic portrayals that existed, Natives had been romanticized beyond any real meaning. Alanis was determined to change people's views.

Obomsawin pushed the boundaries stylistically and told her stories in the way she wanted. Her signature style is the use of subjective intimate testimony from those actually living the story. She has no need for an opposing view to achieve a so-called "objective balance"—the most basic tenet of documentary filmmaking. In her own mind, Alanis was merely redressing a much greater existing imbalance—that First Nations had very little voice at all.

"Her films also reflect a rejection of First World film styles and aesthetics in favour of a more reflexive style which compels the viewer not only to actively deconstruct the issues being discussed but also the filmmaking style they are presented in," said Paul Williams in his article for Senses of Cinema.

Once she had cut her teeth on cultural films in this way, Alanis turned her razor-sharp focus to politics. From then on it's almost impossible to separate her roles as an activist and artist.

Her 1994 film *Incident at Restigouche* was an overtly political slap in the Canadian nation's face. It chronicles two controversial raids by a battalion of 550 Québec provincial police on a Mi'kmaq reserve near Restigouche River. The police were responding to complaints by white fishermen that the Mi'kmaq were overfishing their salmon quotas. The film left few in doubt that so many cops and so much intimidation was an overzealous use of force in the process of "conducting an investigation." Finally, "the other side" was given a voice.

In the film, Obomsawin interviews the Québec Minister of Fisheries, Lucien Lessard, with legendary tenacity. It is never easy to bulldoze a politician. It's harder still to use their words against them, and it's nigh on impossible to get an apology out of one. Alanis managed all three.

She exposed the province's hypocrisy in using arguments to justify sovereignty for Québec that could as easily apply to First Nations. Obomsawin tells Lessard, "When you came to Restigouche, I was outraged by what you said to the Band Council. It was dreadful. The Chief said, 'You French Canadians are asking for sovereignty here in Québec. You are saying it's your country and you want to be independent in your country. We are surprised that you don't understand us Indian people and our sovereignty on our land.' And you answered, 'You cannot ask for sovereignty because to have sovereignty one must have one's own culture, language and land.'"

By the end of the film, Lessard makes a personal apology for any problems his actions may have caused. Against all odds, Alanis' interview with Minister Lessard has gone down in history as one of the seminal moments of Canadian documentary film.

Incident at Restigouche was also important for Alanis in her battles with the NFB itself. She told *Cinema Canada* that her "history at the Film Board has not been easy…Racism and prejudice exist there like anywhere else." As an example, before she made the film, she told the program committee of her plans to interview Lessard. Someone told her that she shouldn't interview whites. She kept quiet and filmed the interview anyway, and when confronted by that same person again later, she declared, "Nobody is going to tell me who I'm going to interview, or not interview. And if you feel that I, as a Native person, cannot interview white people, we'll go through everything the Film Board has done with Native people, and see who interviewed them."

In her next bout with a province over injustice, Alanis even managed to get the law changed. *Richard Cardinal: Cry from a Diary of a Métis Child* (1986) was a sad indictment of the failures in Alberta's child welfare system. The film is the diary of the short but tragic life of a Métis adolescent who committed suicide after being shoved around 28 different foster homes and institutions.

Alanis made the documentary because, as she said in a *Cinema Canada* article, "I want people who look at the film to have a different attitude next time they meet what is called a 'problem child,' and develop some love and some relationship to the child—instead of alienating him."

The film did change attitudes. The Alberta government bought it and screened it to social workers. Alanis recounted her joy at the film's effect on the government, "One time I was in Edmonton…and a man who had been the provincial ombudsman presented me with two new reports, saying that the *Richard Cardinal* film had helped force new policies and laws in Alberta. Young people in the audience said to him, 'Why do you need a film to be made before you change the law?' He quickly replied, 'Well, sometimes the government waits for the public to make a move, to push, otherwise they don't know.' It was incredible. I was shocked but happy that the film was able to do that."

In 1993 Obomsawin became a household name in Canada, but it's likely that not everything said about her was a compliment, because her landmark film that year, *Kanehsatake: 270 Years of Resistance* was tough to digest. In the film, Alanis single-handedly forced the truth about the Oka Crisis onto a nation where many folks preferred to either brush the whole affair under the carpet or swallow the distorted view of the Mohawks as the savages that mainstream media portrayed them to be. The scenario had been played out in Hollywood movies again and again. But this wasn't fiction. This was modern Canada, yet exactly the same thing was happening, and Alanis was there with her camera to expose it.

The focus of the film is the two-and-a-half-month standoff between the Mohawks and the army. Obomsawin was the only journalist left in the mayhem behind the barricades—all the rest were either forced to leave because the Mohawks mistrusted them, or they fled of their own volition as the violence escalated.

The origins of the problem had started months before when the town of Oka decided to go ahead with a planned golf course on a site that was actually a sacred Mohawk burial ground. Barricades were quickly put up, and the Québec police were called in—with tragic consequences. A police officer was killed in a gun battle. The army was called in, and the standoff began.

But according to Alanis, the origin of the problem really started 270 years earlier, when Canada's settlers stole Indian lands. Her film ensured that everyone knew the true context of the struggle— a legacy of historical grievances. On top of that, according to Katherine Monk's article in *Weird Sex & Snowshoes*, Alanis' lens caught "the blatant injustice of the situation that almost every news organization missed, as government and police spin doctors vilified the Mohawk warriors as terrorists with unlimited arms and ammunition. Obomsawin, on the other hand, showed real people behind the bandanas— people who were willing to die for their cause."

Kanehsatake won Alanis 18 international film awards. But for her this was important only because she reached the goal she set out to achieve—to empower her people by telling their story. And this was just the beginning.

Alanis returned to the Oka issue and its fallout in three more films, stubbornly expressing the story from the First Nations' viewpoint. In her latest film, *Rocks at Whiskey Trench* (2000), Alanis reminds everyone who thinks that "it couldn't happen here" that they are very, very wrong.

Rocks at Whiskey Trench follows the shocking events of August 28, 1990, when hooligans threw rocks and bombarded a convoy of 75 cars carrying Mohawk Elders, women and children as they prepared to cross the Mercier Bridge in Montréal. The blatant racism of this faction of French-Canadian men and youths was captured on film and formed the heart of Alanis' film.

Alanis is now in her late 70s, still fighting and still making films. One of her latest, *Is the Crown at War with Us?* (2002), depicts the violence and racial tension between the New Brunswick fisheries and the Mi'kmaq community of Esgenoopetitj.

Obomsawin was born into a culture on the margins of Canadian society, and yet she managed to move into and influence the centre of institutional power. Her work is now accepted by the government she has been criticizing for so many years, and she was rewarded for it. Obomsawin was made a Member of the Order of Canada in 1983, an Officer in 2001 and won the Governor General's Award for Visual Arts and Media in 2001. She also has four honourary degrees and a wall full of other awards.

And Alanis isn't laying down her weapon any time soon, because there are still many stories for her camera to tell. As she said in a *Take One* interview, "In the last 30 years, there has been a lot of progress. They are starting to teach Native languages in universities, but there is so much work to be done. I'm very thankful to the National Film Board for giving me the chance to make these movies because it's all part of the process. I hope things will change and that white culture will embrace Native culture, but I don't think it will happen in my lifetime."

CHAPTER FIFTEEN

Mina Hubbard
Explorer and Cartographer of Labrador
(1870–1956)

She was living in a period of time when it was illegal for a woman to smoke a cigarette in an open car. This was a spiritual and personal journey for her, a way for her to feel close to her husband.

–Waylon Williams,
Mina Hubbard Centennial Committee

SOME PEOPLE WILL DO ANYTHING FOR LOVE. IN 1905 MINA Hubbard raced 900 kilometres through the uncharted wilds of northern Labrador in memory of the husband she adored. She completed the journey as the most celebrated female explorer of her time.

❧

Two years earlier, in 1903, Mina's husband, Leonidas Hubbard Jr., the editor of an adventure magazine, set off to map out a river route through Labrador to Ungava Bay. But a tragic series of events meant Mina never saw her husband again.

The expedition got off to an ominously bad start when the team followed an erroneous government map that took them up the wrong river. When supplies ran out, they turned back, but it was late in the year. They had no food, and the explorers didn't know how to trap or hunt.

Leonidas was too weak from starvation to walk, so his partner, New York lawyer Dillon Wallace, set off to find help. George Elson, another team member, set off in the opposite direction. Five days later, Elson returned to the camp with four Native trappers, only to find a delirious Wallace in the snow and Leonidas dead in his tent.

Mina was distraught and blamed Wallace for her husband's death. She never forgave him, and when he published his version of the tale in a book, Mina was heartbroken once more—Wallace portrayed her husband as a hopeless romantic, a terrible leader and a bumbling fool.

Mina was livid when she discovered Wallace was planning another expedition to explore Labrador. He was going to honour his promise to Leonidas to complete the expedition. But Mina distrusted Wallace's motives and feared more slander. She decided to race against him to see who would get to Ungava Bay first. Mina had never accepted Leonidas' death and privately hoped to either lay his ghost to rest or join him in the wilderness for eternity.

Mina researched and made ready. Friends and family were shocked. She didn't know a thing about the outdoors. The little coverage she received before the trip was mostly a bet on how many days it took before she turned back—just like her ill-fated husband. Derision such as this merely fuelled Mina's determination.

Finally, two years after the first failed expedition, Mina set off with one team, Wallace with another. Her spadework had paid off. Unlike her rival, Mina was well prepared.

Mina had always been a resourceful girl. She was born into the Benson family of farmers struggling to make a living in 1870s Ontario. As a teenager she taught school, which respectable ladies were allowed to do, but then moved to New York to study as a nurse—the only other respectable occupation open to a young woman. As a nurse of 19, Mina took care of an ambitious journalist named Leonidas Hubbard Jr., who had typhoid fever. Leonidas fell for her immediately. When he recovered, he got her a job at his magazine and asked for her hand in marriage.

Mina was thrilled to be out of the typical "female" occupations and was even more delirious to find herself totally and utterly in love. She and Leonidas were married in New York in 1901.

Four years later, Leonidas was dead, but the race in his honour was about to begin. Mina hired a great team to make up for her lack of experience: a Cree named George Elson, the man who had accompanied her husband; Joe Chapies, a Russian-Cree; Joseph Iserhoff; and an Inuk,

Gilbert Blake. They knew the ways of the Native people and the land itself.

Polite society didn't give a hoot that Mina was being accompanied by a group of men with excellent credentials for exploration. All they saw was a wild widow setting off into the wilderness with three wild men. And goodness, there wasn't a chaperone in sight! But the trip wasn't about respectability for Mina; it was about settling old scores.

Mina's team was equipped with food and supplies so they wouldn't have to waste time hunting. She planned for every eventuality she could think of. The four set off on June 25, two to a canoe, with Mina sporting a sweater, short skirt over knickerbockers, a revolver, cartridge pouch and fishing knife—certainly not the usual outfit worn by a respectable widow.

Mina's biggest problem at the outset was establishing her authority. The crew wouldn't let her out of their sight, yet she made it clear that she was leading this group and would not take orders, as the men expected her to and as convention demanded. After all, this was still an era of inequality such that a husband could have his wife committed to an asylum should he wish.

The leader's other concern was that it was one thing to get there, but quite another thing to get back before winter set in. The only way home was likely to be on the last ship out of Ungava Bay.

They were racing against time, with just two months to make the 900 kilometre trip. Not even the Natives knew how long it would take. Mina worried in private, but she never once thought of giving up, though often tempted to do so.

She endured the hardships with stoicism and had no self-pity during the horrors of "fly season," a phenomena that has destroyed the resolve of countless canoeists in those same waters ever since. "The flies and mosquitoes were awful," describes Mina in her memoir of the journey, *A Woman's Way through Unknown Labrador*. "It made me shiver just to feel them creeping over my hands, not to speak of their bites. Nowhere on the whole journey had we found them so thick. It was good to escape into the tent. The next morning I rose early."

And each morning they faced unknown dangers from the wildlife, the strange geography and unfamiliar waters as they inched along an uncharted route through the Naskaupi River Valley, Lake Michikamau and then the George River. The maps Mina drew corrected the erroneous versions of the Labrador river system that led to her husband's death. When her maps were published, they were used for many years afterwards.

As the voyage continued, Mina became more confident with every slosh of the paddle. She discovered herself as well as the land and soon laid Leonidas' spirit to rest among the streams and spruces. She turned out to be an inspiring leader, and George Elson and his team were willing subordinates. Mina used a sextant (an instrument used for measuring the angular distance of objects) to reveal and chart the expedition's location on the map, and the men never questioned the novice explorer's ability.

The expedition was going well, but then Mina heard some terrible news. A group of Montagnais tribe women, who didn't know any better because their men were away trading, told her that they estimated Mina still had a two-month journey ahead of her.

Mina was faced with a terrible choice. Either go on, with the prospect of having to winter in the North for which they were unprepared and ill-equipped, or turn back. She was taking the same risks that had killed her husband, but she couldn't bring herself to go back. Mina chose to believe in herself and the sextant, and the two canoes set off once more.

Ten days later the boats paddled out of river waters and beached on sea mud at Ungava Bay. At last she had completed the journey her husband began. And she had beaten Wallace's team by six weeks.

At a time when women rarely travelled to the North, Mina achieved a remarkable feat. She not only beat a team led by a man, but she was also the first white female to set eyes on Ungava Bay.

James MacLean, a Hudson's Bay Company trader, was the first white man to see it when he made the journey there and back in 1838.

For a while, Canada, and then later the rest of the world, was shocked by the news of this female explorer pioneer. But prejudice still ran rife in the literary geographer's world, and rival Dillon Wallace's account of the race sold more copies than Mina's book.

In comparing the two books, Mina's outshone Wallace's by far, for the accuracy of her maps and the wealth of material she presented—on the land she conquered, the tribes-people she met, and the flora and fauna she cherished. *A Woman's Way through Unknown Labrador* was as much a labour of love as the escapade itself. Mina included her husband's diary alongside her own in the book. The account left no doubt that she would have happily sacrificed her own life to redeem her husband's reputation.

Mina became a novelty as one of the few female explorers in the world, and she embarked on lecture tours across the United States and England to present her findings. People weren't so much skeptical as they were curious.

One man who grew very curious to meet her was Harold Ellis, a wealthy Quaker whose egalitarian beliefs were quite capable of embracing such an independent and adventurous woman. The couple married in 1908 and settled in the United

States, where they raised three children before divorcing in 1926.

Mina often travelled back to Canada and made one final canoe trip on the route she had explored through George River with her age-old friend George Elson.

Then suddenly, at the age of 86, Mina, who by now suffered from dementia, died in an accident that was as surprising as her life—a train struck and killed her on May 4, 1956, in Coulston, near London, England.

CHAPTER SIXTEEN

Naomi Klein
Anti-globalization Guru
(1970–)

*It is important to ask yourselves what you're actu-
ally shopping for. If you are shopping for community, if you are shopping for democracy, you are
actually not going to get it at the mall.*

–Naomi Klein, "Frontline: The Persuaders,"
www.pbs.org

THE *TIMES OF LONDON* NAMED HER ONE OF THE MOST
influential people under 35 on the planet. Naomi
Klein is smart and attractive, feisty and articulate,
and she's got everyone listening—whether they
like it or not—from the youngest sweatshop
labourer in the Philippines to the multinational
CEO in Philadelphia.

Klein is the queen of the corporate backlash, the
scourge of capitalism, the loudmouth spokesperson of the most ardent re-invention of the left
wing political agenda since the 1960s. She is the
guru of the anti-globalization debate; "the chronicler of the first truly international people's movement," as she describes it.

Naomi's brand-bashing book, *No Logo* (2000) has become the modern-day *Das Kapital*, the philosophical glue that unites an otherwise disparate group of activists across the globe, whose only commonality is cursing capitalists. Many environmentalists, third-world debt eradicators, income redistributors, hippies, health freaks and conspiracy theorists believe as Klein does, that corporations are bad for you, and they're on the march, all together, to get things changed.

The reason for Klein's uproar goes something like this. In her book *No Logo*, Klein explains how Nike paid Michael Jordan $20 million in 1992 for endorsing its trainers, which is more than the company paid its entire Indonesian workforce of 30,000 for making them.

This inequality is ludicrous according to Klein, and people are right to be angry. And there's a whole new generation of people, most of them under 30, who sympathize with her and who never even cared about politics before this. The protest isn't against free trade, but it's certainly a protest against how products are made.

Klein and this new wave of activists want to know why corporations seem to operate with impunity in developing countries. And they want to know who really benefits from free trade—the producers or the consumers?

Klein's detractors are many and mighty. CEOs don't like her. At all. She's a pariah to free-market presidents and prime ministers. The *Economist* magazine has led the counter-debate against *No Logo* in various "Pro-Logo" articles that defend globalization as the only way to progress and prosper —while at the same time telling Klein that she needs to grow up.

Toronto was where Klein grew up, though she was born in Montréal in 1970. She remembers her fascination, at the age of six, with neon signs and advertisements, which later developed into an obsession for brand names and, later still, led to arguments with her parents over designer jeans and Barbie dolls. As a teenager she had a job at Esprit because she thought their logo was the coolest. And because she so loved Lacoste, she sewed fake embroidery alligators onto her T-shirts.

This rabid retail therapy was Klein's teenage rebellion against a genealogical lineage of political activists. Naomi's paternal grandparents were Marxists. Her grandfather was fired from his animator's job for organizing the first strike at Disney and put on Senator McCarthy's blacklist. Naomi's American parents moved to Canada in protest of the Vietnam War. They took Naomi to her first anti-nuclear march at the age of 10. She hated it.

When her mother, Bonnie Klein, produced the seminal anti-pornography film, *This Is Not a Love Story*, in 1980, Naomi did not appreciate the attention she received at school—the result of screaming headlines in the *Globe and Mail* that labelled her mother a "Bourgeois Feminist Fascist," and the equally disturbing award of "Asshole of the Month" by *Hustler* magazine. "I found it very oppressive to have a very public feminist mother—it was a source of endless embarrassment," she told the *Guardian* newspaper in Britain.

So Naomi went shopping. "I think it's why I embraced full-on consumerism," she added. "I was in constant conflict with my parents and I wanted them to leave me the hell alone."

Klein's penchant for peroxide and pricey purchases continued until she suffered a massive reality check when her mother had a severe stroke at age 46, just as Naomi was about to go to the University of Toronto.

After taking a year off to care for her mom, Naomi was back at the university in December 1989 when a horrific event changed the course of her life. A misogynist, Marc Lépine, had been refused a place in the engineering faculty of the University of Montréal. In retaliation, he broke up a class, lined up the female students and shouted, "You're all a bunch of f****** feminists," and opened fire. He murdered 14 women. "It was a hate crime against women…Of course, after that you call yourself a feminist," remembers Klein in the *Guardian*.

The newly radicalized Klein turned to journalism and was soon on the receiving end of vehement backlashes for her opinions. She wrote a short article

entitled *Victim To Victimizer* for the student paper.
As a Jew, Klein's opinion "that not only does Israel
have to end the occupation for the Palestinians,
but also it has to end the occupation for its own
people, especially its women," didn't go down
well. The response was a torrent of bomb threats
against her, "and to this day I have never been
more scared for my life," she says.

But even in the face of fear, Klein stood her
ground and decided to attend the Jewish student
unionist's meeting (attended mostly by Zionists)
that was called specifically to plan a response to
her article. Klein has never forgotten that day, saying, "...the woman sitting next to me said, 'If I ever
meet Naomi Klein, I'm going to kill her.' So I just
stood up and said, 'I'm Naomi Klein, I wrote *Victim To Victimizer*, and I'm as much a Jew as every
single one of you.' I've never felt anything like the
silence in that room after that. I was 19, and it
made me tough."

Naomi was a vociferous student activist, argu-
ing about representations of women in the media
and equal rights. She received rape threats for her
trouble. But she was soon disillusioned with this
late-'80s brand of gender and identity politics—it
didn't go anywhere near far enough. So she
dropped out of college and embraced journalism
full time, hoping she could change the world that
way. She took an internship at the *Globe and Mail*
and then an editor's post at *This Magazine*, an alter-
native political paper.

It was during her stint as a journalist that the seeds for Klein's anti-globalization stance were sown. She puts it down to three factors. First, she realized that traditional left-wing politics was bankrupt. Second, she saw serious global issues being simplified and exploited by marketers in order to sell products. Third, the Internet and the global information superhighway had been born. Within this unique convergence of factors, something very new was bubbling.

More specifically, in the early '90s, Klein, *This Magazine*, and the rest of the political left, struggled to find a radically new agenda. The left wing was ideologically battered and bruised after a decade of privatizing Reaganomics in the United States, Thatcherism in Britain and the collapse of communism. Naomi despaired that "The only thing left-wing voices were saying was stop the cuts, stop the world we want to get off. It was very negative and regressive, it wasn't imaginative, it didn't have its own sense of itself in any way."

At the same time as Klein was trying to redefine her political landscape, she was alarmed to discover that the radical issues of the last decade, such as feminism, homosexuality and environmentalism, had suddenly become hip, trendy and hijacked as marketing gimmicks for big corporations. Benetton sold itself as an anti-racism organization, while Starbucks sold politically correct third-world-chic coffee. "I watched my own politics become commercialized," says Klein. It dawned on her that this sort of co-opted advertising imagery was the pseudo kind, but very false-face of capitalism, designed to purposefully mask the more sinister consequences of unregulated worldwide free trade.

So what does a disaffected activist journalist with a bubbling but as yet undefined ideology do? Klein went back to the University of Toronto in 1995. But things had really changed, and she found a "new generation of young radicals who had grown up taking for granted the idea that corporations are more powerful than governments."

Klein was soon clued in to a subtle revolution emerging right under her nose. She watched, sympathized and got in on the act. Her fellow students were a disenchanted generation who didn't vote because they didn't believe politicians would change anything. But what they did believe in was the most effective information weapon ever built—the Internet—and they harnessed its power to spread the new global gospel: corporations were wicked profiteers that had to be reigned in.

Like Klein, the other weapon this group had was eloquence. They were technically savvy and well informed about economics and marketing. If they didn't like something, they researched it and then built a website to distribute their own version and analysis of events.

As a journalist, Klein observed and then wrote about this phenomenon. As an activist, she also took part in the movement itself, helping to create and codify a new global anti-corporate philosophy that grew up alongside the massive multinationals.

As this new grass-roots family was being born, Klein applauded them every step of the way. Soon, the anti-corporate networks mushroomed world-wide, and brothers in developing countries had a platform to tell their wealthy sisters in industrial-ized nations that Shell had polluted Nigeria, and that Disney's CEO made $9783 an hour while the Haitian worker stitching Disney merchandise earned 28 cents an hour. The poor finally had an audience who cared and was smart enough to do something about it. Internet activists chat-roomed, blogged, culture-jammed and agreed to meet at the next world summit.

Klein documented everything she witnessed in a book that later emerged as *No Logo*. She was helped enormously by her famous Canadian TV-host husband Avi Lewis, who hand-delivered rel-evant newspaper clippings to her every morning. Klein first met Avi when she was hired to inter-view him for a CBC TV program in 1993. They were married in 1998.

And what a team Naomi and her husband make. Avi is the charismatic and combative host and producer of the *counterSpin* political debate series on *CBC Newsworld*, where he presided over more than 500 nationally televised debates in three years. Avi's mother, Michele Landsberg, is one of Canada's most renowned radical feminists, who reported for the *Toronto Star* for a quarter century. Should Ms. Klein ever decide to have children, the "radical" in her lineage must be assured, at least genetically.

It took Klein four years to research and write *No Logo*. Finding a publisher, most of which are massive corporations, wasn't easy. In Canada, Random House picked up the book, and in Britain, her only taker was HarperCollins, which was owned by the king of corporatism Rupert-Murdoch's News Corporation. To ensure her anti-corporatist credentials, Klein told the *Guardian*, "What I said when I signed with HarperCollins was that I was going to go out of my way to write about Murdoch, more than I would have done otherwise. I did, and they didn't touch it."

When *No Logo* hit the bookstores, news spread by word of mouth, and sales spread like wildfire, no doubt fuelled by the mass protests, just one month earlier, against the World Trade Organisation (WTO) Conference in Seattle. The event, where protesters stopped delegates from getting to the conference, is now known as the coming-out party for the anti-globalization movement. Forty thousand (the lowest count) took to the streets—a disparate coalition with a general consensus that the WTO favours rich and powerful multinational corporations over the interests of most of the world's population.

Klein was at the WTO conference and described it as the "precise and thrilling moment when the rabble of the real world crashed the experts-only club where our collective fate is determined."

The Seattle protest was exactly the sort of thing Klein predicted in *No Logo*, and the book soon became the manifesto of the movement itself. *No Logo* was translated into 25 languages, was labelled by the *New York Times* as "a movement bible," and was number one on the Canadian and British non-fiction bestseller list for six months. Yet in the United States, it almost wasn't printed due to lack of publisher interest, and then when it was, the book was virtually ignored by the media.

No Logo attacks brands because they symbolize capitalist power gone mad and consumerism with no soul. Logos are no longer guarantors of quality but are designed to sell you a lifestyle—you no longer buy just a pair of running shoes, you also purchase the promise of a healthy existence. The problem is that these products aren't manufactured in a healthy way but are outsourced to the cheapest possible sweatshops in developing countries where companies aren't regulated. Multinationals then become so mighty that they can dictate their own terms—slave wages for workers, environmental destruction and power even greater than governments. If companies don't get what they want, they can just get up and leave.

Klein devotes many pages of her book to complaining that multinationals have taken over
everything back home too. Every available space
in the world has become a billboard—schools,
hospitals, even roadsigns in Buenos Aires are spon-
sored these days. Worse still, brands fuel a never-
ending culture of consumption that has taken over
the collective psyche—people's minds have become
mere marketplaces.

There was an immediate backlash against *No Logo*
from the anything-goes-in-the-name-of-making-
money brigade in business and in the press. Klein
was attacked for being naïve, populist and a hyp-
ocrite. She became the precise type of brand that
she attacked—Klein the trademark represented
aspirations of a win-win, fair and just world for all,
but, claimed her critics, nowhere in her book had
she outlined a practical macro-economic strategy
of how to get there.

Naomi counterattacked that *No Logo* wasn't
intended as a "how-to" economic manual, but
rather a point of debate.

"There is a way for us to respond as citizens that
is not simply as consumers. Over and over again,
people's immediate response to these issues is:
what do I buy? I have to immediately solve this
problem through shopping. But you can like the
products and not like the corporate behavior—
because the corporate behavior is a political issue,
and the products are just stuff. The movement is

really not about being purer-than-thou and pro-
ducing a recipe for being an ethical consumer," she
explained to the *Guardian*.

Klein defends the book as a call to arms of an
increasingly sophisticated activism in response to
an increasingly complex marketplace—the reason
companies don't like these protests is because they
actually work.

As an example, Klein cites what happened to
Nike, which didn't respond to criticisms about slave
wages until a group of black 13-year-olds from the
Bronx (the target market) discovered that they
were paying $180 for a pair of running shoes that
cost $5 to make. The teenagers dumped all their
old Nike shoes outside New York's Nike Town, and
one of them looked directly into the news cameras to warn the company bosses, "Nike, we made
you. We can break you." Conditions in Nike factories are improving as a direct result of the publicity they were subjected to in Klein's book.

Since publication of *No Logo*, Klein continues to
make headlines as the charismatic voice of "the
first genuinely international people's movement,"
as she calls it. She has travelled the world, spoken
at protests and rallies against the International
Monetary Fund and the World Bank, and led
debates attended by a thousand people at the University of New York, with hundreds more turned
away. There is no doubt that more and more people believe Klein's message that anti-corporate

campaigns are "the first baby-step to developing an analysis of global capitalism."

Klein's second book, *Fences and Windows* (2002) is a collection of speeches and articles she wrote in defence of the anti-globalization movement. The "fences" are a metaphor for barricades that block access to natural resources previously owned by the public, such as free water and genetically modified–free food. She attacks governments, organizations and companies for building those fences, as well as the consequent rules and regulations specifically designed to stop people protesting against the "theft." The "windows" are the openings to freedom.

The book was not as much of an international publishing phenomenon as *No Logo*, but it served to develop the anti-globalization agenda, one more baby step forward. And in the interests of equality, she donated all the book's profits to the activist organizations that she wrote about in the book.

Klein continues to be a thorn in the side of the establishment and was one of the earliest and loudest voices to speak out against the invasion of Iraq. In her *Harper's Magazine* article, "Baghdad Year Zero: Pillaging Iraq in Pursuit of a Neocon Utopia," she was one of the first to claim that the Bush administration *did* have a clear plan to rebuild Iraq from the rubble but that it was a self-serving vision to create the best example ever of the free-market economy, built from scratch. Klein lambasted the strategy as one that benefitted for-eigners and their companies exponentially more than the Iraqi people.

Klein is a very busy woman these days, writing her third book and contributing articles for various international publications. And look out world, because Klein is fast becoming the female equiva-lent of Michael Moore and is using movies to doc-ument examples of positive people-power activism. *The Take* (2004) is a feature-length docu-mentary co-produced by Naomi with her husband Avi that chronicles the victory of a group of Argen-tine car-workers who respond to the closure of their auto-plant by taking it over and turning it into a cooperative.

Perhaps the film is just another tiny step forward in the corporate responsibility debate, but there's no doubt that many people are betting that Klein will take giant leaps forward in the future. In October 2005, she was ranked 11th on the list of the world's 100 top public intellectuals in a poll conducted by *Prospect* magazine in conjunction with *Foreign Policy Magazine*. Naomi is only 35, and most commentators would agree that she's got many more years of crusading ahead.

CHAPTER SEVENTEEN

Sarah Emma Edmonds
Nurse and Spy
(1842–1898)

*I am naturally fond of adventure, a little ambitious,
and a good deal romantic, but patriotism was the
true secret of my success.*

–Sarah Emma Edmonds

IF HER DAD HADN'T BEEN SUCH A BULLY, EMMA MIGHT NEVER
have learned the art of cross-dressing. As a young
girl, she impersonated a man to escape an arranged
marriage and her father's violent clutches.

During the Civil War, Emma used her mastery of
disguise to become a "male" nurse in the American
Union army, and then later a spy who crossed over
into enemy territory by masquerading as a black
slave, a female Irish peddler and a cast of other
characters.

Miraculously, Emma's true identity was only
discovered years after the battles were over. By
then she had nearly lost her life more than once
for the sake of keeping her secret safe.

When Emma was born in New Brunswick, Nova Scotia, her father, Isaac, was livid that she wasn't a boy. He already had four daughters, his only son was always unwell, and there was always back-breaking work to be done on his pioneer farm, which he made the girls do. But for reasons Isaac did not wish to discuss, he dressed his daughters as boys and worked them to the bone.

Isaac ruled with an iron fist, yet Emma tried to win his love by being as good as the young man he forced her to dress up as. She became a crack shot, a fearless rider, a stealthy hunter and a badly bruised and beaten up daughter. "In our family, the women were not sheltered, but enslaved," she admitted later.

As Emma grew to despise her despot father, she conversely adored her kind and caring mother from whom she learned the skills of nursing— a plethora of old wives' tales, ancient remedies and ways to heal shattered bones. By the time she was a teenager, Emma had learned an opposing set of skills, one from each parent, that set her up for life.

But Emma found her most influential lesson in the pages of a novel given to her by a travelling salesman. It was the story of a female pirate captain who lived an adventurous life by dressing as a man. Emma took the lesson to heart when her father tried to force her to marry a much older farmer she didn't love. She could either submit and live a life of hell, or rebel and be disowned.

Emma decided to forego the wedding dress in favour of a man's suit. She cut her hair, changed her name to "Franklin Thompson" and fled to Moncton with her mother's help. Emma kept up her disguise so that her father wouldn't find her, and she never set eyes on him again.

For a few years, Emma, living as her alter ego "Frank," became the most successful bible salesman in New Brunswick. Frank soon had so much cash and kudos as a dandy young gentleman that he broke the hearts of many a young lady. The disguise even duped Emma's mother when her daughter returned home as Frank to visit the family while Isaac was away.

Bored with bookselling, Emma went south in search of more adventures. She arrived in Flint, Michigan, on April 12, 1861, the same day as the start of the American Civil War. What better place to test her disguise than to enlist in the army and put her cherished nursing skills to good use to care for wounded patriots? Emma also reasoned that Frank would cause the soldiers much less embarrassment than a female nurse.

It took her four attempts, but the 20-year-old Emma, a.k.a. Frank Thompson, finally fooled recruiters and enlisted as a male nurse of the Flint Union Grays of the United States Army. Luckily, she didn't have to pass a medical, and Frank resembled swarms of other young lads who had lied about their age in order to sign up. Besides, the forces were so desperate for cannon fodder of any age that they often turned a blind eye.

Some researchers estimate that about 400 women disguised themselves as men to serve in both armies of the Civil War. Emma was unique because she was never found out, despite coming close to calamity many times.

On her very first deployment, during the First Battle of Bull Run in July 1861, Emma witnessed the grim costs of war first-hand—men peppered with bullets, surgery floors awash with mud and blood, amputations done by hacksaw, and as many casualties due to non-existent sanitation and poor diet as there were to enemy fire. Worse still, her Yankee regiment was forced to abandon the hospital, and some of the mortally wounded, in a hasty retreat to Washington to avoid being captured by Confederate forces.

Emma volunteered for the additional responsibility of mail courier, which meant she was often away from camp and therefore temporarily relieved of the nightly ordeal of having to get ready for bed in a tent full of soldiers. As a courier, she also became an expert in the surrounding countryside—a vital qualification when the call came for a volunteer spy.

The generals needed reconnaissance on the enemy's artillery and defences before they could launch their next major offensive. Emma wanted the spy's job, so she crammed in as many facts as

she could on weapons and tactics, and turned up
for an interview.

Emma, as Frank, was grilled for hours and was
subjected to a phrenological exam, where the
shape of her head was assessed in the belief that it
determined good character. What the examiners
didn't pick up, however, was that the character
they awarded the job to wasn't a man. Yet in
accepting the job, Emma proved herself every bit
as brave as any man because, if spies were discovered, they were not treated as prisoners of war,
they were simply shot.

"Private Thompson's" first mission as a spy was
to infiltrate the enemy camp at Yorktown, Virginia,
disguised as one of the black male slaves used by
the Confederates for manual labour. Emma wore
a minstrel wig and tattered clothes, and used silver
nitrate to darken her skin. The result was so con-
vincing that men in her own regiment didn't rec-
ognize her. Under the cover of darkness, her new
persona "Ned" made his way toward the enemy
lines. Emma spent her first night out in the open,
trembling with fear.

The next morning, Emma sneaked past the
enemy lookouts and onto the ramparts of fortifica-
tions being built by black slaves. She was instantly
put to work without a second thought. It didn't
take her long to discover that most of the enemy's
firepower was actually fake "Quaker guns"—logs
painted to look like cannons from a distance. Ned

spent the rest of the night wandering about the camp, looking and listening. The next day, he was appointed water-bearer to the soldiers, so he picked up vital clues amid the chatter, about their morale, troop numbers and weapons.

Emma's Ned now had all the information he needed, but no idea how to escape. By a stroke of luck, a rifle was suddenly thrust at Ned along with barked orders to take a shift on lookout duty, with the threat of being shot if found asleep. A nap was the furthest thing from Emma's mind. Instead, while everyone else slept, she ran like hell back to her own camp, armed with her first trophy—an enemy rifle. But the real prize, her information, helped the Yankee generals decimate the Confederates by forcing them out of Yorktown in the next major battle of the war.

Two months later, Emma again transformed herself by imitating her mother's Irish accent and taking on the garb of a fat Irish peddler called Bridget O'Shea. As "Bridget" she embarked on her next mission: penetrate the rebel defences at Williamsburg. She was blessed with the luck of the Irish on this jaunt, though at the start Emma felt cursed at every step.

Her route involved a journey through a mosquito-infested swamp, where she had to spend two nights, and she ended up contracting malaria. Lost, delirious and starving, she eventually stumbled into a house where she discovered a dying enemy soldier. As she tried in vain to save his life, the soldier gave Emma the perfect ruse for entering the enemy camp. In his final breath he asked her to deliver his gold watch to his best friend, Major McKee, in the Confederate camp.

Emma's Bridget struggled to the camp and, looking like a dishevelled and miserable refugee because of the malaria, gabbed her way past the guards. In the time it took to be granted an audience with McKee, she discovered that the enemy had set up a massive trap for Yankee troops. She just had a few hours to warn them.

Emma was in luck. McKee resolved to have his best friend's body buried properly, and he immediately ordered Bridget to ride back to the house with his troops to recover the corpse. When they got there, Bridget was ordered to go on ahead and stand watch. Again, her job as a lookout was her ticket to freedom, and as soon as she was out of the soldiers' sight, Emma galloped back to her own camp. She was chased and took a bullet in the arm but still managed to ride home on her second trophy, a thoroughbred horse she named Rebel. Again, her information was vital in foiling the Confederate's plans for an ambush.

Emma's next spy mission saw her camouflaged as a black mammy who broke into the rebel camp and was put to work in the officers' mess—a blessed place to collect tidbits on the latest battle plans as the officers debated their strategy over their meals.

As if that stroke of luck weren't enough, the next day, when doing the laundry, Emma found a bundle of papers in an officer's coat that outlined the battle plans for the enemy's capture of Washington, DC! It was time to get out of there.

This time, escape wasn't guaranteed. Although Emma slipped easily out of the rebel camp, she walked straight into a major battlefield. She hid in a house, which, minutes later, was reduced to smithereens by a cannon ball. When the fighting eventually died down, Emma crawled out of the rubble and inched her way back to her own side with the bundle of papers. When her superiors digested the significance of the bundle and how it could foil an enemy advance on the Capital, Emma's "Frank," who was back in the ranks as a soldier, was hailed as a hero.

Emma's most dangerous mission was also her last as a spy. Dressed as a rebel prisoner, she was discovered behind enemy lines by a Confederate captain named Logan. Thinking Emma was a young man on the run, Logan threw her into the rebel army, and the next day she was on a battlefield, facing her own comrades.

Faced with the irony of being shot by her own unit, Emma held back when the cavalry charge sounded until there was so much confusion on the battlefield that she could gallop back toward her own regiment. She was recognized by her own unit's commanding officer, who tried to guide

Frank back to camp. But, just yards away from safety, Captain Logan caught up with her. They both drew pistols. They both fired. Logan fell. Emma lived, but her cover as a spy was blown.

Frank's superiors decided it was too risky to send "him" spying again so Frank was put to work sniffing out spies in their own camp. Emma uncovered three of them, who were all shot, thus cementing Frank's reputation as a legendary intelligence and surveillance agent.

But just as Frank's military star was rising, Emma was brought back down to earth with a jolt. In 1863 she was struck down with another bout of life-threatening malaria and faced with the dilemma of either exposing her secret or leaving the army to find private treatment as a woman. She chose the latter, fully intending to return to the ranks if she recovered. She survived the malaria but was devastated to discover that, by then, Franklin Thompson had been added to the list of army deserters.

Emma didn't tell a living soul about her secret, nor did she reveal the truth of Frank's gender identity in print when she wrote a memoir of "his" adventures entitled, *Nurse and Spy in the Union Army*. The book was a bestseller, but she donated the profits to charities for wounded soldiers and humbly served out the rest of the war as her real self, nursing in military hospitals.

When the war ended in 1867, Emma was homesick and returned to New Brunswick where she met and married Linus Seeyle. The couple settled in the United States, where they raised three sons of their own and fostered many orphaned black kids, two of whom they adopted.

But Emma couldn't rest until she had cleared Frank's name as a deserter. She decided to tell the truth in 1882, in the hopes of also securing an army pension. It took two years and a lot of detective work for Emma to ferret out her old military colleagues. Once they got over the shock, they testified that, yes indeedy, oh my goodness, their old comrade Frank, was the very same Emma Edmonds Seeyle.

Finally, in 1884, a special act of Congress granted Emma Edmonds, a.k.a. Frank Thompson, an honourable discharge and a $12 monthly stipend from the U.S. army.

Emma was honoured as the only woman granted membership in the Grand Army of the Republic, the organization formed by Union veterans after the Civil War. She happily spent the rest of her days with her husband, living, ironically, in the formerly Confederate state of Texas, where she is buried in the military section of the Washington Cemetery in Houston. Her epitaph reads simply, "Emma Seeyle, Army Nurse."

CHAPTER EIGHTEEN

Cassie Chadwick
Con Artist
(1856–1907)

*I would not like to live another minute if I did not
think I could pay these poor people back.*

–Cassie Chadwick

SHE POSSESSED EYES THAT MESMERISED, CHUTZPAH WITHOUT
limit and such a gargantuan obsession for money
that she was blinded to any scruple—perfect qual-
ifications and characteristics for a con artist who
became the most notorious swindler of her age.

Cassie Chadwick had no intention of living the
mundane life she was born into, so she set out to
enrich her own world by any means necessary. In
trying to get her grubby little paws on other people's money, she started young, stealing from her
siblings. She graduated to forgery, fraud and prostitution, posed as a clairvoyant and ultimately
passed herself off as the heiress to America's
biggest fortune.

She was a low-life who lived the high life. For
a while she was filthy rich, living on dirty money,
yet she was toasted and fêted by the crème de la
crème of aristocratic society. But crime also cost

Cassie a great deal—she died alone in prison, penniless and without remorse.

❦

Elizabeth (Cassie) Bigley was born in the small town of Eastwood in southwestern Ontario, around 1856. Even as a young girl, Cassie couldn't keep her hands off other people's stuff. Almost as soon as she could walk, she exasperated her sisters by incessantly stealing their clothing and jewellery. If anything went missing in the Bigley household, it was Cassie who had invariably stashed it somewhere.

It was clear all too soon that the lifestyle afforded by Cassie's railroad-worker father would never be good enough for her—she wanted cash, and lots of it—so at 11 years old she tried to sell her father's gold watch to the local barber. Not even a trip to the police station to explain herself, nor her father's wrath, was enough to scare the young girl out of a future life of crime.

Cassie was at it again, just a year later, arrested at the tender age of 12 for trying to pass herself off as an heiress. She stood trial on charges of forgery and fraud but successfully pleaded insanity and was released.

For the next 10 years, Cassie kept a low profile, until she popped up in Cleveland, Ohio, again posing as a wealthy woman. She successfully duped Dr. Wallace Springsteen into marrying her in 1880, but 11 days after the wedding, Wallace discovered she had lied about her future inheritance and had the marriage annulled.

Accounts of the next 10 years vary. One version states Cassie had a son, Emil Hoover, by another Cleveland husband who died a few years after their marriage and left her $30,000. Another story claims Emil was the product of her life as a prostitute.

Many accounts corroborate that Cassie changed her name to "Madam Lydia De Vere" and posed as an elegant noblewoman to whom unsuspecting gentlemen could safely lend money. Wrong! Alternatively, "Lydia" masqueraded as a clairvoyant who used her hypnotic eyes and a variety of ruses to extricate extremely large sums of money from any sucker she found.

All reports agree that in 1889 Cassie was arrested for defrauding money in a Lydia De Vere psychic scam. She was sentenced to 10 years imprisonment in the Ohio State Penitentiary for her cash-conjuring tricks, but the governor pardoned her after three and a half.

Prison did nothing to reform this voraciously greedy impostor. After her release, Cassie ensnared Dr. Leroy Chadwick of Cleveland, a wealthy widower with one daughter, by using the same heiress-posing rip-off as before. Leroy and Cassie were married in 1897. But this time, Cassie had a plan—a plan that led to the most sensational swindle in North American history.

Soon after the wedding, Cassie engineered a trip to New York, where, by chance, by sheer coincidence, she just happened to "accidentally" meet a lawyer friend of her husband's, Mr. Dillon, in his hotel lobby. Cassie requested Mr. Dillon chaperone her on a ride to her "father's" home, to which he readily agreed.

When Cassie gave the carriage driver her "father's" address, Dillon was incredulous. He recognized it as belonging to Andrew Carnegie, one of America's richest men. Too polite to say anything, Dillon's eyes almost popped out of his head when the buggy pulled up outside the massive mansion and Cassie made her way to the front door.

Cassie breezed into the house and managed to string out her visit for half an hour as she spun a long yarn, first to the startled butler and then to the housekeeper. Cassie said the purpose of her visit was to check out the references of a servant girl she was hoping to employ. When the housekeeper claimed never to have heard of the young lady, Cassie merely apologized for the inconvenience and left, but she made a great show of waving goodbye as the door closed behind her.

Dillon's mind was racing. Could it be that Andrew Carnegie was Mrs. Chadwick's father? Or was she visiting someone else? As Cassie stepped back up into the carriage, she supposedly tripped and "inadvertently" dropped a piece of paper. Dillon picked up the note for her, and as Cassie purposely fumbled, he had time enough to read the piece of paper. It was a promissory note from the multi-millionaire Carnegie himself for a colossal chunk of cash—$2 million!

Dillon's shock was met with Cassie's feigned shyness and her pseudo-demure admission that she was indeed Carnegie's illegitimate daughter. Poor little bastard. Dillon could hardly breathe when she confessed that "father" often gave her sums as big as this. Besides, she added, $2 million was paltry in comparison to the $400 million inheritance that would soon be hers. Cassie begged Dillon to guard her secret with his life.

Dillon was so discreet the news spread like wildfire, and every banker in Cleveland soon courted Cassie to open an account. They lent her ludicrous sums of money at ridiculously high rates of interest. To pay off the interest on each loan, she simply borrowed from another bank, backed by another forged promissory note, in an endlessly inflated cycle of spending money and acquiring more loans.

For the next six years Cassie spent millions of dollars of other people's money. She once threw a party that cost $100,000 and frittered away thousands of dollars on hundreds of dresses that filled 30 closets. She squandered a small fortune on a gold piano for her living room and once, on a trip to Toronto, spent thousands on jewels in a single store. If she went to New York on a shopping trip, she rented a private car on the train. She travelled

first-class on her annual expedition to the bou-
tiques of Belgium and Paris, which, of course, was
de rigueur for a lady of such fine standing.

The rich and famous from Cleveland to Europe
had Cassie Chadwick on their Christmas card and
party invitation list, and no one asked any questions, not even Cassie's husband. Until, that is,
Cassie borrowed $190,000 from a millionaire
Boston banker, Herbert B. Newton, who had the
audacity, a few months later, to ask for the interest payments on the loan be paid back on time, as
agreed. Cassie missed a couple of instalments, and
Newton grew suspicious enough to check out her
financial situation with fellow bankers in Cleveland and New York.

Within weeks Newton discovered that Cassie
was millions of dollars in debt. When he demanded
his loan back, in full, immediately, Cassie couldn't
pay a penny of it. He responded with a lawsuit.

In the scramble that followed, it was discovered
that Cassie Chadwick had deposited $28 million
worth of "promissory notes" signed by Andrew
Carnegie in various banks across the country.
Every note was a forgery, and the old man issued
a statement saying that he had never heard of
Cassie Chadwick, nor in the last 30 years had he
signed a promissory note of any kind.

When the swindle hit the headlines, customers
from every bank that had loaned Cassie cash
dashed to retrieve its savings. The Citizens National

Bank of Oberlin, which loaned her $800,000, was besieged with such a big run of withdrawals that it collapsed completely. Yet, even as innocent investors were losing their livelihoods and their homes, Cassie claimed her innocence and promised to repay her debts.

The people of Cleveland suddenly made the connection between Mrs. Cassie Chadwick and the pseudo-psychic Madame De Vere, who had been convicted 10 years earlier. Cassie was eventually arrested in a New York hotel, allegedly with $100,000 in her belt.

As the creditor's clamour for Cassie's blood reached a cacophonic pitch, poor Dr. Chadwick, who had been on holiday with his daughter in England, returned home. He was arrested at the dock and also charged with fraud, but was quickly released due to lack of evidence. As the criminal's husband, however, he was responsible for her debts and lost everything, including the inheritance he planned to bequeath his daughter.

On March 10, 1905, Cassie was tried in a Cleveland court for the biggest hoax in America's banking history. She was charged with seven counts of conspiracy against the government and conspiracy to wreck the Citizens National Bank of Oberlin. Cassie was jeered throughout the hearing, and a roar of approval went up when she was fined $70,000 and sentenced to 10 years, once more at the Ohio State Penitentiary.

After years of luxurious living, Cassie fared badly in her damp, dark prison cell, but she ended up serving only two years of her sentence. According to one newspaper article, "She fretted incessantly over her confinement until it became almost impossible for her to sleep. At times she was so peevish the patience of the prison officials was sorely tried."

Three weeks before her death in 1907, Cassie collapsed into a delirious state from which she never recovered. Her son, Emil, was summoned to her deathbed but arrived a quarter of an hour too late. Cassie passed away, alone.

The headline in the *Toronto Globe* read, "Ontario Girl Who Caused a Sensation in Financial Circles Three Years Ago Dies Far From Any Friend in a Foreign Prison."

The Ontario girl had travelled a long way from her humble beginnings to the top of the social ladder, and all the way down again. It was a mean feat in an era where husbands owned their wives and a wife's greatest attribute was her virtue and her modesty—two qualities that Cassie Chadwick lived and died without.

Notes on Sources

Common Sources

Butts, E. *She Dared: True Stories of Heroines, Scoundrels and Renegades*. Toronto, ON: Tundra Books, 2005.

Forster, M. *100 Canadian Heroines*. Toronto, ON: Dundurn Press, 2004.

Rosella Bjornson

Render, S. *No Place for a Lady: The Story of Canadian Women Pilots. 1928–1992*. Portage & Main Press, 1992.

Cassie Chadwick

Crosbie, J.S. *The Incredible Mrs. Chadwick: The Most Notorious Woman of Her Age*. Toronto, ON: McGraw-Hill Ryerson, 1975.

Women in History. *Cassie L. Chadwick*. Lakewood Public Library, www.lkwdpl.org/wihohio/chad-cas.htm.

Anne Cools

Braithwaite, B. & Benn-Ireland, T. *Some Black Women: Profiles of Black Women in Canada*. Toronto, ON: Sister Vision: Black Women and Women of Colour Press, 1993.

Wente, M. "Anne Cools, Renegade." *Globe and Mail*. Saturday, March 1, 1997.

http://sen.parl.gc.ca/acools/english/biography_e.htm

http://www.egale.ca/index

Dr. Tana Dineen

Dineen, T. "Blaming the Boys." *Peace Magazine*, Dec 1986/Jan 1987, p. 27.

Milstone, C. "On the Couch." *National Post*, Ontario. 5 March 2001.

Sauer, M. "'Renegade Psychologist' Dukes it Out with Feelings Folks." *Union-Tribune Newspaper, USA*, November 25, 1997.

Sarah Emma Edmonds

http://www.civilwarhome.com/edmondsbio.htm

http://www.pinn.net/~sunshine/whm2002/edmonds.html

Rose Fortune

http://www.coolwomen.org

Pearl Hart

Markle, D.E. *Spies and Spymasters of the Civil War*. New York: Hippocrene Books, 2000 (1994).

Penny Hoar

Kaplan, B. "Penny Hoar." *Toronto Life Magazine*, August 1994, Vol. 28, No. 11.

http://www.walnet.org/csis/people/penny_hoar

Mina Hubbard

Holmlund, M. & Youngberg, G. *Inspiring Women: A Celebration of Herstory*. Coteau Book and the Saskatoon Women's Calendar Collective, 2003.

Klondike Kate

Lucia, E. *Klondike Kate: The Life & Legend of Kitty Rockwell: The Queen of the Yukon*. Hastings House Publishers, 1962.

Dr. Frances Oldham Kelsey

Bren, L. "Frances Oldham Kelsey: FDA Medical Reviewer Leaves Her Mark on History." *U.S Food and Drug Administration FDA Consumer Magazine*, March–April 2001.

Mel, J. Frances Kelsey: Invalidating Thalidomide for Prenatal Use. http://collections.ic.gc.ca/heirloom_series/volume6/218-219.

Naomi Klein

Klein, N. *No Logo: Taking Aim at the Brand Bullies*. Vintage Canada, a Division of Random House, 2000.

Klein, N. "Baghdad Year Zero: Pillaging Iraq in Pursuit of a Neocon Utopia." *Harper's Magazine*, September 2004.

Viner, K. "Hand-to-Brand-Combat: A Profile of Naomi Klein." *Guardian Newspapers Limited*, Saturday, September 23, 2000.

"Who's Wearing the Trousers?" *The Economist* print edition, September 6, 2001.

"Why Naomi Klein Needs to Grow Up." *The Economist*, November 7, 2002.

k.d. lang

Lemon, B. "k.d.: A Quiet Life." *The Advocate*, LPI Media, Los Angeles, June 16, 1992.

Scott, J. "k.d.: Chatelaine's Women of the Year in 1988." *Chatelaine*, January 1988.

Sloan, B. Transcript of *Sixty Seconds Extra*! Interview with k.d. lang, September 27, 2004.

http://groups.msn.com/langisms/kdmagazinesads.msnw

Alanis Obomsawin

Beard, W. & J. White. (editors). *North of Everything: English-Canadian Cinema Since 1980*. Edmonton, AB: University of Alberta Press, 2003.

Harewood, A. "Alanis Obomsawin: A Portrait of a First Nation's Filmmaker." *Take One*, June–September 2003.

Monk, K. "First Takes: Our Home and Native Land." In *Weird Sex & Snowshoes: And Other Canadian Film Phenomena*. Vancouver, BC: Raincoast Books, 2001.

Steven, P. "Interviews: Alanis Obomsawin." In: *Brink of Reality: New Canadian Documentary Film and Video*. Toronto: Between the Lines, 1993.

http://www.collectionscanada.com

http://www.sensesofcinema.com

Ada "Cougar" Annie Rae-Arthur

Horsfield, M. *Cougar Annie's Garden*. Nanaimo, BC: Salal Books, 1999.

Manon Rhéaume

Hill-Tout, W. *Manon Rhéaume: Woman Behind the Mask*, TV documentary produced by The National Film Board of Québec, 2000.

Rhéaume, M. with C. Gilbert. *Manon: Alone in Front of the Net*. Toronto, ON: Harper Collins, 1993.

Nell Shipman

Blakeman, C. "The Girl from God's Country: Nell Shipman and the Silent Cinema." *Take One*, December 2003.

Drew, W. www.welcometosilentfeatures.com, 1997.

Foster, G. *Women Film Directors: An International Bio-Critical Dictionary*. Connecticut: Greenwood Press, 1995.

Shipman, N. *The Silent Screen and My Talking Heart: An Autobiography*. 3rd ed. Boise, Idaho: Boise State University Press, 2001.

Zemel, J.H. *Nell Shipman: A Brief History*. www.svpproductions.com/nellshipman2.html. 1997–2002.

Emily Stowe

Ray, J. *Emily Stowe*. Don Mills, ON: Fitzhenry and Whiteside, 1978.